The Walk
My Journey of Survival of the Japanese Military Occupation of Manila

The Walk:
My Journey of Survival of the Japanese Military Occupation of Manila

Ruth Hale Cobb Hill

Donald Wayne Downey, Editor

Donald Wayne Downey
Denise Lorraine Armstrong-Downey
2016

First Printing: October 2016

ISBN 978-1-63010-004-9

Front Cover Photo: Hale Family estate in Sta. Ana with Ruth's mother's house (back left), Main House (center) and five rattan factory buildings (right).

Dedication

This is dedicated to all the brave men and women
who helped my family and me during the war.

Contents

List of Figures in Appendix

Acknowledgements

I wish to express my warm thanks to my old friend George Wagner, colleague and Veteran of the Korean War, who passed on a couple of years ago. He told me of Pedro Pineda, a Filipino war veteran, who invited me to contact Cecilia Gaerlan, a relative of his, a woman who is very interested in the history of the Bataan Death March. She introduced me to the work she is engaged in, which is to lobby for the inclusion of Philippine WWII history in books used in California schools. Her project led to the formation of the Bataan Legacy Historical Society. I thank her and all those who volunteer for giving us WWII survivors the opportunity, through the Conference, to share our stories, thus making it possible for us to learn more truths about ourselves, as well as inform younger generations.

I also give thanks to Memorare Manila 1945 for keeping intact the stories of how individuals and families survived the destructive rage of the retreating Japanese Military, especially during the last battle for Manila. I thank Rod Hall for sharing with us his extensive collection of books about WWII in the Philippines. I give my deep appreciation to my dear friend Connie McHugh, his sister, who, along with him, lost loved ones but survived, showing us how to face the future. She is active in helping the Bataan Historical Society pursue their ambitions, and we have shared with each other many stories of our experiences of the war.

I thank the Philippine Consulate General of San Francisco for supporting the platform of the Conference, thus influencing the material presented.

I give thanks to Mr. Jintaro Ishida, author of "The Remains of War: Apology and Forgiveness," a former officer with the Japanese Navy, who searched for me to offer his regrets after having seen the destruction of Calamba by the Japanese Military. He and I corresponded for a while.

I give thanks to the townspeople of Cuyo, Palawan, who told me of how my uncles, Alfred, Andrew, and Paul, formed the Cobb Guerillas, and how the Japanese made only one visit to Cuyo and left immediately, so no harm was done there.

I acknowledge the staff of the American Historical Collection at the Rizal Library of the Ateneo de Manila University. They furnished me with my grandfathers' concentration camp information. They also gave me materials about my grandfather, Frank H. Hale's businesses and his place in Philippine society.

I acknowledge the staff of the Lopez Library, who gave me materials from their Frank H. Hale business and Masonic files.

I thank Joseph Henderson and Jean Shinoda Bolen who listened to my stories for years as I tried to purge myself of them by metabolizing my experience. I thank Lory Campos and Evelyn Wanta for their encouragement and support. I give deepest appreciation to my husband, Gareth, for his patience during times when remembering war events became trying. I value highly, the keen pursuit of my personal history that my son, Anthony, and daughter, Lorna, exhibit in relation to my war stories. I thank Jovan and Xavier, my growing grandsons, who listen hard, taking in as much as they can. It has taken me about three years to put my war stories together. I extend my appreciation to Angeleen Campra who patiently edited as I went along.

Introduction

In the summer of 2016, I was invited by the Bataan Historical Society to be part of a panel in a conference they were holding in the fall. Our panel was asked to present about our life experiences during WWII in the Philippines. I accepted, not giving it much thought. As I prepared for it, however, I came to a realization that I always found it difficult to write about the war. From the time we were liberated in 1945 from the clutches of the Japanese Military, I would jot down notes about incidents I recalled. The thoughts in these notes were usually without beginnings or endings. They were simply random. I had stacks of them. Then I would get rid of them, not knowing why. They seemed important at the time. I would go to World War II books, especially those with pictures. Those brought about heavy feelings, but I never associated those feelings as coming from a place beyond my consciousness. Sometimes my thoughts and feelings were so tangled I had to isolate myself and quietly unravel them. I did not want to share them. As a result, I had no encouragement. I did save some of those "beginnings," thinking that someday I would get back to them and begin a task of amplification. Instead, I stopped writing about the war altogether.

A time came, when I was teaching Tagalog at UC Berkeley, that I found myself rewriting those "beginnings" in the Tagalog language. I was surprised to find myself producing streams of thoughts that had coherent beginnings and endings. All of them were about the war. I began to analyze them through a psychological filter. I realized that the Filipino side of me was the active speaker. I wondered what happened during the war that made this material one-sided. I am half Anglo-American and half Filipina. What happened to my American side? Was it repressed? Did I lose that half of my identity altogether? What did the Filipina side have that made her able to speak? What conditions brought about this identity shift, beyond the trauma of war and having to survive physically? I spoke more openly in Tagalog, but not sufficiently. I was frustrated by not being able to bring together both sides. I did not, or could not, work on it. I have decided it is time to write about that of which I had not been aware.

There are certainly many books that focus on the history of the war. My task is to write about my own experience, perchance to become more conscious of what I repressed during the war. I have an intuitive feeling that my discoveries will have an impact on persons, who like me, were born of intermarriages. Certainly it will have meaning to my descendants.

Chapter One
Anticipation of outbreak of the war

I am half Anglo American, half Filipina from both my paternal and maternal sides. I lived with my maternal grandparents, Frank H. Hale of California, USA, and Teodora Elazegui Hale of Calamba, Laguna, Philippines. They were owners of the ESCO Hale Shoe Company, the largest shoe manufacturer in all of Asia prior to WWII, the maker of the famous ESCO shoes.

In our home in Sta. Ana, Manila, the war was anticipated by my grandfather, Frank H. Hale, who, asked by General MacArthur to prepare a location to house medical equipment and supplies, to serve that area of Manila if needed, closed his rattan factories, railroad line, and dry kiln along the Pasig River, and repaired landing docks to carry heavy material. My grandmother anticipated by interpreting-two red sword-like appearances in the sky which she said she had seen before the Spanish-Filipino War which left her an orphan. This was all taking place when the Japanese military's descent from Manchuria was beginning to feel ominous.

I was 9 and in the 4th grade in Central School, the elementary school section of H.A. Bordner School in Taft Ave., Manila on December 8, 1941, when rumbles of army trucks and sirens filled the air, beginning a pandemonium I had never seen before. An army truck stopped and an officer rushed into our school saying to his teacher-wife that we were at war, that Pearl Harbor had just been bombed, and that they were on their way to Pampanga. Classes were stopped, parents were called, the principal, teachers and staff packed records, and sadly, we were all saying goodbye to each other, not knowing what lay ahead. My mother, in an act of bravery, drove her limousine and chauffeured students to their homes. I had not seen her with this initiative before. In private, she told us that grandpa was coming home to Sta. Ana from the shoe factories in Paco to inform us, including staff from the factories, of his plans and strategies.

Grandpa had already been preparing for the possibility of war, saying that Japan was forcing its idea of its racial superiority on all, and we would have to prepare to keep the light in the ensuing darkness. Proceeding to practical matters, he said that General MacArthur seemed hopeful that every citizen could and would rally. We as a family would stay together including the people working for us if they so desired. We would not arm ourselves, for God had not meant for life to be lived that way. We would speak truthfully always. We were the head of a large conglomerate, and our workers would need protection and support. We, the family, took his humanitarian words as carrying moral authority. As a child, I felt I had to grow up fast.

A phone call came from Papa Olsen, our beloved caretaker of our Baguio properties, who said that Baguio had just been bombed but he and Mama Olsen were fine and would hide in the woods if need be. I felt his strength and fatherly warmth. Rather than be left with fear, I felt I could let go of Baguio in my thoughts for now. I worried though, for President Quezon, who was there, a neighbor, whom my Grandfather and I had visited that summer in his tiny library as he was taking care of his health problem—tuberculosis. Will he be safe? How will he protect us all?

That evening, explosions from the bombing of Nichols Field, not far from us, began. The skies were red from flames. We were hoping our planes would outnumber the Japanese planes. But, Nichols Field was annihilated. We, as a country, were unprepared. The knowledge of this was where real fear came from.

For protection, Grandpa ordered the roofs of the factories painted with Red Cross signs. Air raid shelters were built at our compound, at the factories, and in Pandacan where many employees lived, using leather scraps instead of sand. ESCO acted faster than the local government did.

My mother and my siblings, who lived in another house in the compound, moved to our house. My father was in the US. My mother buried his guns, family records, and anthropological material in gasoline drums under *santol* (sandoricum Koetjape) trees. We were in blackout, and windows were taped. Hiding was paramount, as we did not yet know what our enemy was like. Within the next few days, our house was strafed. We could not run to our air raid shelter and hid instead, in a storage closet under five stories of concrete.

We were informed, possibly by the American Consulate, that we would be evacuated. We were to wait for a boat to arrive at our dock, taking with us only the barest essentials. The boat never arrived. This scared me and left me feeling abandoned.

An oil company close by blew up its stock, so that the Japanese military could not use the oil. Manila was preparing for possible takeover. My grandparents decided it was time to evacuate. My mother instructed a caretaker to be liaison with my father's family in San Juan. We loaded up all the children under mattresses in a couple of trucks (which we thought was fun) and went to the Binangonan Church in Binangonan on Laguna Bay, where Australian priests welcomed us to stay in two rooms that were used as storage rooms for icons.

There, I woke up at 4:00 am to the sound of church bells. I did not know what it was about. Except for funerals and weddings, I had never gone to a church. Out of curiosity, I sneaked out our room, tiptoeing through a creepy hallway and down the stairs, through heavy 18th century doors, out to the church garden, and through a side door into the church. Altogether, there must have been about a dozen people inside. Some were kneeling. A ritual was taking place and, with the beautiful organ music and incense, I was moved. I sneaked back to my cushion before anyone else was up. The following morning I did the same thing. When I came back to our room, my grandmother confronted me, saying that she knew where I was going. I explained to her that what I was seeing was so beautiful that I wanted to do it again, especially the receiving of "something" (communion) that seemed to make people so peaceful. She said she would have to think about it. Later, she said that I would have to take lessons.

My grandmother was the daughter of revolutionary Filipino parents, who died fighting in a skirmish with Spanish colonial soldiers who had forced them to give up their land, leave their town, and to walk into the jungle. Orphaned at a very young age and left to care for a younger brother, she learned to survive, with the help of a childless aunt and uncle, but mostly with her instincts. Gathering all she could of what she heard from the elders, she learned to read the signs in the heavens—for instance, whether the Big Dipper was empty or not—and she developed a wisdom and capacity to see, born of this relation to nature. She learned how to heal the soil and the sick and to create beauty and bounty. She was a strong, gentle woman of the land, and through her, I participated in her worldview. And, she protected me. Because of her negative experience with punitive Catholic priests and nuns in Calamba, where she grew up, she never identified with religion. This was a point of connection between my grandparents. They had been refused marriage by the local Spanish catholic priest because he condemned intermarriage, and they had to go to Batangas, where they were married by a Filipino priest.

My Grandfather was openly critical of the Catholic Church, especially after cleaning up a dungeon as a volunteer after the Spanish surrender during the Spanish-American War. My grandmother saw Christ as a symbol, just as a tree might be a symbol of God. From her, I learned to humble myself to nature and to have an open attitude about those whose natures were unknown to me. She taught me that observing nature at its deepest core brings one to an understanding of the souls and fates of people, animals, plants, insects, and children. She often said that I pulsated in a different rhythm, and she questioned how it was that I came into her life—perhaps by chance, but mostly as a gift. We bonded deeply, with her watching our movements closely, correcting the light and dark within us and the universe.

Her husband, my Grandpa Hale was from Northern California and became a very wealthy industrialist in the Philippines, who upheld a belief in human dignity and equality. His beliefs and actions led to his being characterized by some as a friend of the Philippines and the Filipino people. He had grown up on a northern California ranch, where he learned to make boots and saddles. He mastered this craft of shoemaking for the US Army while being on a ship with Commodore Dewey as a civilian volunteer, sailing from San Francisco to the Spanish-American War in the Philippines, and later at an army shoe repair shop in Fort McKinley, made possible by General Pershing, who observed that soldiers' military shoes broke down very easily. He engaged immediately with Philippine tanneries and suppliers, insisting on the quality that he needed, opening up a new way for Philippine shoemakers to make shoes. He was able to get the Fort McKinley authorities to open up its gates to Filipinos, who wanted to come to his shop. His motto became "Replace the *chinela* (slippers) with shoes." ESCO became the largest shoe manufacturer in the Philippines, and possibly in all of Asia according to an economist as reported by the American Historical Collection at Ateneo de Manila University. This was made possible by the use of new machinery from Boston that enabled production in large numbers, enabling exports to the US and Europe.

He became strongly imbued with the philosophy of Scottish Masons and became a Grand Master of the highest ranking Lodge in the Philippines to which some of the most powerful men belonged, including President L. Quezon. I was in awe of my grandfather's personality. He was a humanist with powerful and heroic masculine energies. He was fearless, honorable, good at defense, and stalwart in the midst of change. He taught me the principles of justice, integrity, and equal rights. He was my tie to the West and its brand of ego consciousness.

Calamba, from where my Grandmother came had a number of Masons who had joined in Europe. Jose P. Rizal, the Philippine's national hero, was from Calamba, who became a Mason in France. My Grandmother was close to his family, and knew about Masonry through him and others in Calamba. This was another connection between my grandparents.

I looked forward to going back to Manila to get lessons about the Church. While we were in Binangonan, however, Grandpa stayed in Manila. He had ordered retirement pay to be given to all the employees, the factory clinic put on emergency basis, and the bank accounts to be distributed to employees before confiscation. None of his employees would be unprotected. The daughter of the clinic doctor, now a psychologist, to this day attests to the quick measures ESCO employees took in return, in spreading their individual charity to others.

Chapter Two
Interrogations, Concentration Camp and Hiding

The day after Christmas, Manila was declared an open city, and my grandparents decided to face the realities of meeting the Japanese army on the ground. There was fear of the Japanese entry into the city, especially because there were rumors that atrocities had been committed. Philippine and American troops and nurses left for Bataan and Corregidor. President Quezon and General MacArthur were either in Bataan, Corregidor, Australia, or the US; we did not know. We were now on our own.

Our handsome, elegant Japanese gardener tearfully bade us goodbye, confessing that he had been a spy. Japanese spies were suddenly appearing, and in contrast, many Japanese families who lived for long periods of time in the Philippines reached out to help Americans, including us.

Americans were arrested and taken to Santo Tomas University in Sampaloc, which was turned into a concentration camp for Americans. Filipina wives were not taken. My grandmother and I could see that this was set-up to demoralize Americans, and to deceive Filipinos of the promise of their own freedom as long as they followed Japanese sovereignty. Marriage between East and West was not acceptable. This was very obvious in the way they talked to us.

Every day, we were visited by cars full of Japanese officers with fully armed soldiers who interrogated us about our racial and national backgrounds. They did not take my grandfather to camp right away. My Grandpa Hale resisted saying that the factories were already being prepared for an independent Philippines and questioned the Japanese right to take over what was already being geared to become a Philippine company. Japanese officers could not and would not answer his question.

As if from nowhere, a Japanese Colonel, asked if he could live in one of our rental houses right across the street from us. His cook, who was half Japanese and spoke Japanese very well, asked if he could cook at our house and if the colonel could dine with us every day, for breakfast, lunch, and dinner. My Grandfather guardedly extended his welcome. They were very cordial and formal to each other. During this time, not a single Japanese Military person came to our house. The Colonel loved to hear my piano playing and after lunch he and my Grandpa would quietly listen to me. We bowed to each other before he left for his nap. One day he announced that he was leaving, to go back to the front, in spite of the fact that he disliked war. He thanked me for my piano playing and showed me a picture of his family back in Japan.

After leaving the house that he took over, officers came back to our house in groups that included lawyers. The Japanese lawyers emphatically stated that everything belonged to the Japanese military. A civilian group was flown in from Japan to take over and run ESCO, with the help of ESCO employees. Workers, after the war, reported that the military did not run the factory. They also took over the rattan factories with the medical supplies, as well as our Lyric Music House in Escolta. Only then was my Grandfather taken to concentration camp.

Chapter Three
Massacre and fire in Sta. Ana

My Grandmother, being Filipina, was not taken to concentration camp. My grandparents made a pact that while he was in camp, she would hide with the children. And indeed, I was hidden. Being white, I hid behind heavy damask draperies when the soldiers came, standing on baseboards so my feet would not be seen. I hid myself anywhere I could, depending on the situation. New officers and soldiers came, confiscating everything they could get their hands on. My mother became defiant and insisted that her things were hers, ripping off seals right in front of the soldiers. I was scared for her. We began to give away things and hide stuff in friend's homes.

One evening, after the soldiers had left, I became aware that I was turning—vigilant, a feeling I did not like. I worried about it as I thought it was not healthy. I was beginning to loose appetite for food. I ate dinner quickly, excused myself and went upstairs to my room to be alone, quiet, and prepare for my evening bath. Climbing up the stairs felt good, as I slid my hands on the heavy smooth wooden banisters, listening to my sibling's voices fade as I became more solitary. My sister, Grace, followed me and asked if she could bathe first, and I said she could. When she came out, I went in, and took a long hot bath, calming down, getting ready for a good night's sleep.

I came out the bathroom into my room in my pajamas, expecting Grace to be in her bed next to mine. The room was eerily quiet—Grace was not there. I walked in to the partially opened stained glass doors that separated our bedroom from the library wondering why it was opened, and to see if she was out there. A shock went down my spine and I slid on my knees as quietly as I could under my four poster bed. I felt stupid as I knew I was visible. My spontaneous response to the shock was to hide, but a four poster bed offered no place to be invisible. My mother and my siblings were lined up against the library wall, looking scared and grim. A Japanese soldier was in front of them holding his rifle and bayonet at them. I knew that if he had any idea that I was behind him in the bedroom he would shoot or bayonet me. My time had come I thought. In a split second I said goodbye, looked up and said to whoever was up there, maybe God, who I never addressed this way before, "I am with you now." At that moment, my mother lunged at the soldier, disarming him from his gun which fell to the floor. He was caught by surprise. She told him to behave himself as she went back to the wall. He straightened up and obeyed her. At the same instant, soldiers came running down the stairs from the roof garden and floor above in their cleated boots, carrying guns and machine guns. The soldier in front of my mother and siblings ran down with them, and as he did, fell down the stairs, dragging his gun and bayonet. I ran to my mother and siblings who were surprised to see me. We all laughed a freaky nervous laughter, as we shook ourselves from our near death experience. Immediately, machine guns began firing outside. People were screaming, and we could tell when their lives were cut off by bullets. We laid flat on the floor, wondering if there were any more soldiers in the house. My siblings whispered to me that soon after Grace left the bathroom, soldiers came into the house and ran up to the roof garden where they started shooting at looters who were ransacking for medical supplies at our rattan factory turned medical supply station next to our house. Within the thick concrete bathroom, I did not hear a thing. My mother was made to line up the children against the wall in the library, and a guard took over to make sure they were not to stop their work of massacre. Soon it was silent. My brother Frankie crawled to the veranda door and opened it slightly. The killing was audible, as well as the sound of bodies being thrown into the Pasig River behind our house. The soldiers then boarded trucks and left. We were all numb and speechless.

Our guard, who was from India, beat on our door; we found him wounded, proceeded to nurse him, and called the town doctor, who walked from his house, hiding himself behind fences and rock walls. The guard said, "I didn't see them coming; they were hiding behind the trees and bushes and attacked and tied me up." Clearly this was not the work of just a few soldiers, but was ordered from a higher command. Rather than guard the place, they wanted to show the power they had. The next morning our angry, camouflaged handy men insisted on going into the factory grounds to survey what happened and found body parts, a body on reeds on the side of the Pasig River, and one in the back of a building. A woman came to us insisting she be escorted around because she was sure her husband was there, and she found him. City officials arrived, were horrified and said they would take it up with the Japanese Military, but did not know where to report. The whole matter died down, leaving the whole of Sta. Ana feeling scared and oppressed.

A few nights later, I woke up to a huge fire outside my window; the factories were burning. It looked as though it were just outside the window panes. I could feel the heat. We wrapped ourselves up and were led by our men out of the house and down to an empty field across the street. We laid down on blankets, watching the inferno which fire engines tried to put out. My grandmother said, "I thought we already lost everything, but fire makes sure everything is gone." Neighbors came and stayed with us. Fortunately, our house did not catch fire. I was thankful that the fire would end the violence. To have continuous murder was horrifying. The clean-up of the debris after the fire took a few days and was done mainly by the Manila Fire Department. The Japanese military didn't seem to care what happened. No one ever figured out how the fire started.

Chapter Four
Hiding

Two buildings out of seven survived. The Japanese Military moved in one building, turning it into barracks for Japanese soldiers resting from their tours in Bataan. They built a huge hot tub outside. We knew that these soldiers would not be leaving the premises for a while. They were extremely raucous, and we were afraid of them. My mother and grandmother got very concerned that with these soldiers around, the women in our household might not be safe. I, in particular, white and now nine years old, stood out. So, as the soldiers were moving into that building, my mother and grandmother decided to hide me away from Sta. Ana. I was to move immediately to the Drake's house on Calle Herran near Concordia College. The Drake sisters were my grandmother's very close friends. I was smudged all over with mud and, wrapped like an old woman, was made to lie on the floor of a *carretela*, a horse-driven vehicle, along with a case of milk and a sack of rice. The *cochero* (coachman) and I went past the Japanese soldiers, with me crouched on the floor. As soon as we got past our gates and onto Old Panaderos Road, I could breathe again. I realized I had been holding my fear in for weeks.

Going to the Drakes was always a treat for me. Evelyn and Lory, their grandchildren, were like brother and sister to me. I felt very lucky that I was going to their house. They had two armoires that were full of toys. I always looked forward to playing with them. That night was very strange. I talked and talked all night, and Evelyn kept giggling, happy that I was there. We could not sleep. The house, adjacent to Calle Herran, was tightly shut. We stayed indoors never opening the front door nor windows. The following night we allowed ourselves to peek through cracks in the windows to see what the rumbling was on the street; it sounded like very heavy trucks. Unfortunately, we did. Passing by were army trucks full of dead people. We thought they must have come straight from Bataan. They were being taken to the Sta. Ana Race Tracks, where they were burned. A huge fire was going on in that direction and we could smell the burning bodies. We also heard screams. We wondered if some of the dead were not completely dead.

My mother and grandmother sent us news every day. The Japanese soldiers in the barracks from Bataan were rotated. New soldiers kept coming in. All of a sudden the rotation stopped and a smaller group remained. Our family was getting used to their presence. The soldiers were not bothering the family and respected the boundaries between our family grounds and the rattan factory grounds. My grandmother, my mother, and my Aunt Christina who lived across the street from us wanted me back. This time, I would have to live with my Aunt Christina. The Japanese never showed interest in her house. It was probably because she was married to a Filipino. Once more, I was smudged with mud and rode on the floor of a *carretela* to my aunt's house. There I stayed upstairs only, as the first floor was visible from the street. I played with my aunt's shoes and perfumes. I felt very isolated. Feeling sorry for me, my aunt allowed me to sneak out with her once. Bundled up and looking like a Filipina, I went with her to the Sta. Ana public market. It was incredible to be out. One day, I decided I would go out on my own, went to the backyard and climbed under a barbed wire fence. I went across the field we had taken, thinking I could make it all the way to the market. I suddenly got cold feet and came back. As I was reaching the fence, I saw a Japanese sentry near the house, and I could easily be seen. I crept all the way to the back, scratched under the barbed wire fence to crawl back in, only to find my aunt's bulldog staring at me. He had been trained to be a watch dog, and I was afraid he might not know me. I looked at him and decided that I would have to take a chance with him and kept on digging. "Puppy" came to me, licked my face, enabling me to quietly get back into the house. I locked all the doors, and with a sigh of relief, thanked God that I was saved.

We noticed that there were fewer Japanese soldiers in the barracks. My mother said she missed me very dearly and wanted me back home. Again, I was smudged and bundled. This time, being watchful of when the sentry was around or not, I walked back home alone. There I stayed indoors all the time. Being at home was a little scary. I watched out the window every now and then just to make sure that none of the soldiers came into our area.

One exception occurred. A young Japanese soldier, about 18 years old, would come to our garden and ask my mother's permission if she would allow him to play with my baby sister in her or a maid's presence. My mother trusted him. He would come for about ten minutes every day to hold my two year old sister. She smiled at him and got to know him. One day I decided to come out of my hiding, and when he was playing with her, I came out and joined them. I smiled at him and he smiled back at me. He was not even surprised to see me. I knew instinctively this man would not hurt or betray me. I felt some divine intervention going on and believed there was something greater than us then. I shall never forget him.

Soon after, we were notified by Japanese officers that we had to leave, that despite the fact that my grandfather was in concentration camp and that he was married to a Filipina, she did not have the privilege of staying in the house. Our friends, the Rustia family, who had a house on the beach in Pasay told us of a house that had just been vacated near them. We arranged to move immediately. Leaving was very sad. Before we even had a chance to vacate, the Japanese brought in their contractors to transform the house into an Officer's Club, and hung up a huge Japanese flag from the second floor balcony. We felt very humiliated.

Chapter Five
Introduction to a changing Manila

Preparing to leave our home at 85 Old Panaderos Road by the Pasig River would have been impossible had we not held a deep faith that we would be coming back to it when the war was over. We did not know what the future held for us. The house was the center of communication for the entire family and extended clan-from the USA to Cuyo in Palawan, in the southern part of the Philippines, where my father's side of the family settled at the turn of the 20th century. It was also the center of communication among the employees of the various Hale enterprises. These businesses were now confiscated by the Japanese Military.

News we used to hear through radio was now stopped. All our radios were confiscated. Telephone lines were cut. By now, communication was through letters and word of mouth. As a consequence, more people came to our house for news. Newspapers were available, now full of propaganda about Japanese military successes against America. They were also full of admonitions to the Filipino people to appreciate what the Japanese had done, that they saved Filipinos from American imperialism. "Asia for Asiatics," the new slogan, was broadcasted. Simultaneously, new regulations had to be strictly observed. Communication was no longer what we had known it to be. Manila was becoming silenced, and suppressed.

Relatives on my maternal grandmother's side from Calamba, Laguna, urged us to move there, where we would be under their protection and where we would probably have connections with the underground. But Grandma insisted we stay in Manila where we would be closer to Santo Tomas Concentration Camp where we might be able to get news of Grandpa. We took food to him daily, leaving it with American internee volunteers at the front gate, to give to him. Occasionally we were able to send notes to him through a doctor who was permitted to go in and out of camp, until the doctor himself was barred from going in.

On trips back and forth to Santo Tomas, we began to feel the tightening of rules, both from the guards at the gate and from sentries scattered all over Manila. A lot of cruelty was brought upon people who they felt needed to be taught a lesson, such as not bowing low enough, or lighting up a cigarette in front of sentries. People were slapped and humiliated publicly, or punished by having to stand in the sun for hours, or interrogated at police stations. Some were taken for severe interrogation and punishment at Fort Santiago, in the old walled city of Intramuros. Just hearing about this place frightened people. I was not allowed to leave the house.

Our move to Pasay meant we were cut off from my father's family in San Juan, which was now far and dangerous to get to. We were worried about my Grandpa Ira, my father's father, who lived there and was suffering from Blackwater Fever, having been bitten by a deadly mosquito at his ranch in Dumarang, Palawan, just before the war. My Aunt Ruth, his daughter, and her husband, also being harangued by the Japanese military, had taken him to the Hospicio de San Jose where he was cared for by the Sisters of Charity. When the Japanese found him, they moved him to Remedios Hospital in Malate, Manila, which was commandeered for old, sick Americans and other nationalities. He was registered as an internee of Santo Tomas Concentration Camp. My mother was informed by the hospital that he was there and she was allowed to visit him once. She was able to tell him that his sons, Alfred, Andrew, and Paul left Manila for Cuyo, Palawan. (Known as the Cobb Brothers, they formed their guerilla group and worked with other groups. Alfred escaped with another American on a Moro *vinta* (a sailboat used in Mindanao) to Australia where he met General MacArthur. Paul was killed in Cuyo. Andrew stayed with other guerillas.)

The move changed our lives completely. Our family, including my aunt's family now lived in a house barely large enough for all. We lived dormitory style, with beds very close to one another. As the eldest girl among my siblings and cousins, I began caretaking of the younger ones. My aunt had two maids stay with her, as they could not go back to their families in the Visayan Islands. All of our male helpers, except the former driver, sought other jobs.

A Catholic school, Sta. Rosa College, opened a branch in our area. We enrolled only to be told within two weeks that because of our American names, the Japanese Military would take us away. The nuns advised my mother and aunt to keep their children indoors as bands of Japanese soldiers patrolled the streets. During the short period at the school, I learned a lot about everyday Philippine life that I had not been exposed to before, such as singing Philippine songs, dances, weaving, and reading in Tagalog. I also began the study of the enforced Katakana, basic Japanese appropriate for our ages. Soon after we stopped, we heard that Japanese soldiers came to the school to inspect student roles.

Formal schooling had come to an end. We had very few books at home, published in the Philippines. Books published in the US were banned. Friends hid most of our books for us. To own them was risky. In public, English was spoken less and less. I found myself becoming more expert in Tagalog, which I enjoyed, loving hearing what was called "deep Tagalog". This was the Tagalog spoken in Laguna where my Grandma Hale was from. I read everything I saw—pamphlets, prayer books from a nearby chapel, even leaflets, propagandas—I felt I needed to know everything that was going on. I was unconsciously shifting from being a protected child, whose early years were devoted to education and culture, to a child whose instincts were readily accessible, and the pursuit of safety was primary. At home, I became teacher to all the younger children, while I studied arithmetic.

I began to get curious about our neighbors. Never had I been in close proximity to neighbors, so I introduced myself to them when it was appropriate. Our block had large houses, which were gated. The atmosphere was formal, the families well-to- do, and obviously pro-American. What we shared was news, about the battles in Bataan and Corregidor, and whether any of their male relatives were coming home from ongoing battles or not. I also learned that men of the Chinese families had been taken away by the Japanese Military and that the families were still waiting for their return. An old dowager Chinese lady across the street allowed me to visit her. She looked and dressed like an empress, with tiny feet and very long painted curling nails. She sat on a dais in her elaborately embroidered robe. The room was heavy with incense. She never smiled, but asked me to take a sip of tea. Her husband had been taken away. I knew she was hurt and angry. I said I would see her again. I was also impressed by how many of these families were quite wealthy, owning elegant horse driven wagons copied from those of Victorian England. They were called *dokars*. These replaced cars, which were now used only by the Japanese Military.

I read recipe books and experimented with cooking. We had no power a lot of the time, so we did not save food—everything had to be fresh. At 4:30 in the morning, I would get up and walk to the beach to meet lone fishermen bringing in their catch. I was joined occasionally by market fish vendors. I learned all about each catch—different fishes, crabs, and shrimp. I bought those that were still alive and freshest. I made soups, fish salad, fish mousse, stuffed and baked fish. I became very creative, and got accolades for my contribution to the meals. It was fortuitous, as food prices had gone up very high, and fish at the beach was still cheap.

In March, we were informed by the Santo Tomas Concentration Camp authorities that Grandpa Hale was sick and needed an operation. He was given permission to go to the Philippine General Hospital where his physician, Dr. Sison, would perform the operation. We were so glad he would be out of Camp, albeit temporarily. He was to wear an armband, identifying him as an American. He would also have to check in with authorities every week. He was picked up from Camp in an ambulance with an emergency doctor. He felt so guilty being in an ambulance, knowing that sick and dying men in Bataan and Corregidor had no help. He said he would take a *carretela*, a horse driven vehicle, but was too weak to resist. Two days after he arrived at the hospital, Dr. Sison operated on him. I was there with Grandma from daybreak to nighttime. I volunteered to help nurses pass water to burn victims, who lined the corridors and balconies. It was the first time I saw casualties of war in great numbers. I got instructions from a nurse and a social worker. Japanese officers and their interpreters checked in on Grandpa a few times during his stay. The nurses would tell me to hide when they saw them coming. Dr. Sison was able to get permission from Santo Tomas authorities to allow Grandpa to convalesce outside concentration camp, and instructed us as to how to take care of him. He came home with us. Dr. Sison gave me a certificate for my services.

In the following days, General Wainwright, top Commander of the US and Filipino forces surrendered to General Homma in Corregidor. This was celebrated in Manila by the Japanese Military, with a parade that included loudspeakers announcing Japan's superiority. Few people came out to witness the parade, except for employees of companies who were ordered to attend. Manila was quiet. American men were paraded in states of disarray while American women were made to watch them go by. I saw Grandpa's eyes well up in tears. I, on the other hand felt angry, and ready to fight, if only in my imagination. Grandma asked for news from Calamba, if they had heard from her two nephews, one in the US Scouts, and the other in the Philippine Army. They were both in Bataan, and the Death March. News came to us later that both died in prison camps, one in Capas, and the other in Camp O'Donnell.

In a week, my mother was informed by Remedios Hospital that Grandpa Cobb had died and she was to come and sign papers. He died of a heart attack after having eaten a banana and taken a walk. His address was listed as Ateneo, the University which had a famed telescope that he used as a hydrographer and weather forecaster. His other address was the Hospicio de San Jose. My mother was the one in the family who was called because she was the wife of his eldest son. She sent a courier to Aunt Ruth in San Juan.

Aunt Ruth took charge of the funeral, helped by her sisters-in-law, the siblings of the former Speaker of the House, Eugenio Perez. The incredible number of Commonwealth government politicians who attended demonstrated loyalties to the US. Even though the services and funeral were solemn and quiet, the whisperings and handshakes attested to allegiance to America, incorruptible faith and strength. The past month's humiliation was uplifted with what seemed like a toned down fighting spirit. Some men put the American flag over his casket as we prayed "Our Father," distinctly a western prayer. It was immediately removed, folded, and given to my mother, the wife of the eldest son. The funeral cortege was very long and full of *dokars*, contributed mostly by the Taberra family. The procession wound its way from Funeraria Nacional in Sampaloc to San Juan Parish church. He was buried in a crypt on an outside rock wall in the churchyard, fronting beautiful flowerbeds.

Grandpa Hale was too weak to attend. He stated his goodbye by saying that it was better that Grandpa Cobb died before the war got worse. In San Juan, Aunt Ruth was preparing to bring her whole family to the Ilocos provinces, where her husband had property. She was bringing Lola Petra, my paternal great grandmother, who was nearly 100 years old, as well as Aunt Esther, her sister, and her family. We did not see them again until after the war.

As soon as he began to feel better, Grandpa Hale became very concerned that the food available to the people was of inferior quality. He had hoped that more protein could be introduced in the daily diet, using peanuts as a staple along with rice. Braving the Japanese soldiers walking on the streets, he put on his arm band and walked daily to San Andres, to the Bureau of Plant Industry to introduce his idea to Miss Orosa, the Plant Directress. The two began experimentation with peanuts. He went there every day and a collegial relationship developed between them. The peanut experiment was successful and the next step was to implement their findings. Unfortunately, Grandpa was informed he had to go back to Concentration Camp. Miss Orosa followed up as much as she could. Towards the end of the war, Miss Orosa was executed by the Japanese military. Before going back to Camp, Grandpa made two "shoeshine" boxes. He gave one to a street boy who he felt would use it to make a living. He gave the other one to my brother Frankie who was ashamed of it, thinking that Grandpa did not think he could do better.

Soon after Grandpa went back to Santo Tomas, the owner of the house we were renting announced that the Japanese Navy had commandeered all the homes on our block for the Navy's use. Grandma hired an agent to look for a place big enough for all of us in as inconspicuous place as possible. The agent found an abandoned university dormitory on a street right behind the Santo Tomas Concentration Camp back gate, on Calle Asturias. Since the university had been converted to a concentration camp, the dormitory was empty. We moved in as fast as we could. My remembrance of Pasay has stuck in my mind, particularly of a lovely Mayday celebration called Flores de Mayo in a chapel on F.B. Harrison Street where we little girls brought flowers to lay at the altar.

Chapter Six
Behind the Concentration Camp

The neighborhood had its blessings. The Santo Tomas Chapel, which was retained by the Dominican Priests, was open to the public. Right next to it was the university gym which was converted by the Santo Tomas authorities as the old men's internee housing. From the chapel grounds, this area was open, and except for a barbed wire fence, the gym ground was visible to whoever went to and from church. As we walked slowly to and from the chapel, we would see Grandpa go in and out of the gym for meals at the main campus. He recognized us and almost every day we would have sight of each other, even though we masqueraded our looks. One day he was hit by a Japanese guard as he picked a leaf from a bush. It was devastating to witness, but he walked on. We could tell he was not going to let the incident get to him.

In February of 1944, this area was completely walled off from the chapel grounds. The atmosphere in Manila was getting tense. Food was scarce, with the Japanese Military confiscating everything that came in from the provinces. Food was rationed even in the markets. Prices went up, and people were beginning to starve. They were selling off their jewelry, furniture, clothes, in order to afford staples of rice and corn. Bartering became common. A new market arose for this purpose in Bambang, not far from us. People were carrying coffins on their backs to take to burial places. Sickness pervaded. There was no medicine to buy. The numbers of spies for the Japanese rose and people were being taken to torture places for questioning. We were feeling the lack of food, as we had to ration among ourselves the little we were allowed to buy. I became an astute buyer of food and became very good at making food stretch. We began to mix rice with other starches to stretch the staple.

My recourse to the hardship was to play the piano more and more, cut out paper dolls, and build doll houses. We memorized plays and made our own versions of characters. We held shows and recitals and made the grown-ups the audience. We met other families with children. Asturias Street became a lot of fun in the afternoons after the sun went down. We played *patintero* (a Philippine game similar to kick-the-can), hide-and-go-seek, and the neighborhood version of soft ball. We were included in a community fiesta, where I became a character called "Justice" and had a chance at putting on real make up, not mud. When we had a flood, the boys made rafts and played in the water—yuck!

Japanese soldiers were getting aggressive, running over people on Lakon Laan Street, which was a major thoroughfare. One casualty was a Chinese man whom the driver pulled out from under his truck and threw into a garbage pile. They also started walking outside the concentration camp. Unbeknownst to me one day, I was followed by a Santo Tomas Concentration Camp sentry. I walked slowly but directly to the apartment of a woman physician, who opened her door immediately and let me in. She had seen what was happening. She and I watched him leave. Then I went home, just a few houses away.

In September, 1944, a lot of us children were playing on Asturias Street near the street corner just outside the back gate of the concentration camp. All of a sudden, US reconnaissance planes flew low above us, followed by a dog-fight. They were so close, we all ran home. A blast took place right behind us. Two Chinese boys living at the corner of Dapitan and Asturias lingered. The planes disappeared as rapidly as they came. My brother and I ran to the corner as we were worried about the brothers only to find their beautiful bodies bloodied and dead. Their hysterical parents were running towards them as well. I wondered if God could not have given them a chance to live longer. This raid marked the beginning of a quiet *zona* on our street.

A *zona* was the closing of a street for the purposes of investigating the people who lived in it. With the raid, people were beginning to talk about the possibility that Americans were about to come back. This led to the appearance of a stranger, possibly a Filipino spy, on our street. That same week an apartment house that had seven male residents were inspected. All seven were taken away in a Japanese military truck and never seen again. The stranger lived in a small house in an alley off of Asturias Street. The male head of another house was taken away. The strange man began to show off new clothing and would strut up and down the street with a sense of power that scared people. There was talk that he might not just be a spy but also a *Makapili*, a pro-Japanese person who would, without conscience, divulge pro-American people. At that time, everyone was a nationalist and felt close ties to America.

Early one morning at 5 am, my Uncle Albert, my mother's 15 year old brother, opened the upstairs front window, climbed up on the sill, looked over the gate of Santo Tomas and shouted "Grandpa." I ran to him to see if he indeed had seen Grandpa. I caught sight of the strange man standing in front of our house, looking at us. Albert, a budding defiant teen-ager shouted at the man saying, "Your day will come!" I slammed the window shut and told Grandma of what just happened. Because of the preceding happenings on the street, Grandma decided that we all needed to leave Manila before men in our household were also taken. We hired a coconut fueled vehicle and took very little with us. We boarded around 4 am the following morning. I was smudged all over with mud. A couple of men, probably guerillas, helped the driver wait for the optimal time to cross past the sentries at the sentry-post in Balintawak. This post was centrally located to watch for transportation going to different provinces. We were going north to Baliwag, Bulacan. The sentries inspected our vehicle and were more interested in the vehicle than the people in it. They let the driver go. We reached an old friend's house located on the main road. It was an ancestral house turned into a museum. The owners, the Magno family, welcomed us to stay in that house. They lived in a modern house close by. In Baliwag, we had more access to food as well as freedom. It was quiet where we were and we became acquainted with some townspeople. We also learned that there were spiritualist churches in the area, mostly in the woods. This captured our imagination and my brother and I tried to snoop in their windows only to be asked to leave. By November, we were hearing rumors that Japanese were seen in the main road, retreating from Manila to Baguio.

Chapter Seven
Escape to Barrio Labak, Pampanga

Early one morning there was a knock on our back door. A man, a stranger, said in a hushed way that it was getting dangerous on the main road, that the Japanese soldiers were burning houses. We were to follow him, and that many of the other families in Baliwag were leaving. He said, "Do not bring anything." I woke up the family, making sure all my siblings were in order, and grabbed a bottle of water. Grandma, followed by my mother and then us, followed him into the woods. Past the woods was an open field where many different families were already congregated. My aunt's husband's brother who had been a mayor of Baliwag divided up which families were to go, and with whom. There were 115 in our group.

The chill of the morning air made my asthmatic siblings noisy with their sneezing and wheezing. The men carried them. Then we were all silent, like shadows going through jungle paths. We reached the open fields and walked on rice paddies. We had no food. All we had was the bottle of water I grabbed as we were leaving. We rationed that among the younger children. We headed for the Rustia's country home, where we arrived at 8 pm. More men joined us as we were walking. One of the Rustias identified them as guerillas. At the Rustia's, we had bowls of *lugao* (thick rice soup) and slept like sardines on the floor. I, myself, had no place to sleep so I slept on a stair. Early the following morning, after a breakfast of more *lugao,* we walked to Barrio Labak, at the foothill of Mt. Arayat in Pampanga. At this point, we were only one third of the original 115 as others were led to other barrios. We were very exhausted. Strange men took turns carrying my siblings on their backs.

On the way there, there was a dog-fight between an American and Japanese plane not far from us. The American plane got hit and the pilot parachuted. Grandma asked a couple of men to run and look for the pilot to see if they could help him. That afternoon, news got back to us that the pilot had just been killed. We did not know how and by whom. There was not much reaction from the strange men with us.

We arrived at Barrio Labak late at night and occupied a tiny two room *nipa* hut. *Nipa* is a type of grass used for roofs of huts. They belonged to a tenant farmer of the Tiongson family, who owned the rice fields. There were two huts, and the farmer moved to the hut next to ours. Ours was right in front of an irrigation ditch. The following morning we were so glad to see mudfish in the rice fields as well as in the ditch. We had quite a feast of rice and mudfish. We learned the farmer's way of living, planting, harvesting, winnowing, separating the rice from its husk, grinding to smoothen the rice, and storing edible rice in jute sacks. Every evening was marked with singing and serenading with guitars, followed by *lugao*.

It was in this field that I met the leader of the guerillas we were with. He was the famous Luis Taruc, leader of the Hukbalahaps. The Hukbalahap used to be a radical, peasant movement in pre-war days. It rose to become one of the most successful guerilla groups during the war. Its social outlook was different from non-radical groups. They were opposed to the Japanese, but to the landlord as well. We had some scary times.

My brother Elmer who was a blonde one year old, and my cousin Earl, two years old, were playing on the ground alongside the irrigation ditch. I was watching them from the window of our hut. Out of nowhere three men on horseback approached. One of them was pulling the American flag on the ground. The leader looked fierce and said to the boys, "You Americans, you will have your day." The boys, crying, ran to the hut and I ran to meet them. The men disappeared as mysteriously as they arrived. Upon inquiring, we found out, the name of the leader was Kidlat, meaning lightning.

My aunt's husband, a Tiongson and landowner, went to Taruc who lived in a small house about a half a kilometer across a paddy from us. Taruc sent word to our family that he would not allow anyone to harm us. I was curious about the mysterious goings-on. Once, when all of us were bathing in the beautiful Pampanga River, we noticed some of Taruc's men watching us, as though guarding us. A stranger came and told us in whispers, to go home because there were other guerillas across the river watching us too. It was rumored that another guerilla company, was on that side of the river. The *magsasaka* or tenant farmers were warm, gentle people, always ready to care for us.

(Eighteen years after the war, while on a visit to my family in the Philippines, I was invited by my Uncle's brother to go with him on a campaign trip to this area. He was running for mayor again. He wanted me to bring my son, a blonde three year old, with us. I brought American food as gifts. The elders were gone. The huts were now houses made of concrete blocks. A small store supplied the tenants with extra income. A strange man picked up my son and put him on the back of a *carabao*. My son became a farmer for the rest of the day, picking up rice stalks and stacking them up. He loved it. This visit was interpreted by the tenant farmers as my way of giving thanks to them for what they had done for us during the war. This form of reciprocity is expected in the Philippines. It assures that connection is kept. My uncle's brother was well liked and supported these tenants as they were seeking recognition as legitimate guerillas after the war. He won the election.)

Chapter Eight
The Walk

It was before the sun was to take its course to becoming hot as the noon day sun, and our hut was becoming filled with it. I felt exasperated—one more day of sameness—hunger and illness creeping up; the sore on my left ankle shin was not getting well, and I thought I was beginning to smell it. This began a process of associations to poor people in the streets of Manila—most of them with sores and infections, no medicine, no food—when Albert came running, with his great big eyes looking like he had seen Heaven, towards our hut, and I arose immediately. He had been running for guerillas—not officially, but with dedication and fervor—after all, he was just a young man, not much more than a growing boy. He wanted so badly for Americans to come back; he shouted, "The Americans are here!" Shock came to me—not so much that the Americans had arrived but that my soul was immediately filled by a gift, the return of men who would fill me up again with some kind of masculine spirit I had missed for so long. I ran to Grandma; she grabbed her little pocketbook, and off we were, leaving everyone else behind and running after Albert, who was leading us to where he saw the Americans.

It was quite a journey from Barrio Labak in Pampanga, in the rice fields where we were, in the foothills of Mt. Arayat, to where we were going. We were not sure where we were going, but we were met by some villagers and guerillas, who said in encouraging voices, unlike the muffled ones they had spoken with the last four years, that indeed they heard shots and tanks, that the Americans were on the main road coming from the north. The shift in my heart, from that of yielding to my fate, perhaps to death, to rapid beating and an excitement I had not felt in years took me to the main road, where I saw a miracle of men in khaki green, carrying guns on their shoulders. The smell of khaki was strong. I could not believe what I was seeing and smelling. They were burned by the sun. Their helmets were not large enough to protect them from nature. Whoever designed their helmets thought of bullets, not knowing how nature also took its toll. Their heavy boots were covered with the Philippine mud and dust I had become very familiar with. I was breathing in what I saw. Yes, they were back, the promise that was made was kept. God's grace was back in force with me.

Grandma sent word back to our hut, through a villager whom she paid, that she and I were going to Baliwag, back to that town, and that my mother and aunt should look for someone who had a *carabao* and wagon, or a *carretela* to bring the family back to Baliwag. Albert went on ahead of us—tagging along on the side of the road with the soldiers—and the last I saw of him, he was pointing to a dead body, warning that I should not step on it.

A soldier saw me, a white girl, and looking stupefied, asked me, "What are you doing here?" I struggled to bring my voice to my mouth—I had not heard English in so long. I was about to cry but held it in answering, "I am from here. This is my grandmother." He looked at my Filipina grandmother, and, with a slight bow, kept going ahead.

As we walked, I held my tears back, as I knew I was saying goodbye to the placid rice fields I had come to love. We were in war, and these men were here to kill, tromp on the evil, as it was the only way, I thought. I wondered if I would ever see the *magsasakas* again. Yes, I would come back and repay them for their hospitality, their kindness, and the bravery they mustered to keep us safe.

A rifle shot followed by a couple more—someone was dead for sure. Guerillas around scurried in its direction. An American Captain signaled to his men to continue their walk. I knew they were headed for Manila. The dead on the sides were Japanese soldiers, being pulled by guerillas and soldiers out of the way and piled up for trucks to take away. I felt very small, a bystander, being strong. Walking was invigorating. Tiredness did not mean much, even though I was limping sometimes.

We reached Baliwag and headed for the house we were living in on the main road. It was not burned, although others were. The troops kept their march on the road—it was endless. We had been walking for hours. As I was opening the gate, an officer came to me, handed me a small can of ham and said, "Cook this, I shall be back tonight." I was dumbfounded, but took the can of ham. He looked back and waved at me and I waved back. Feeling so slow in my heart and mind, I momentarily imagined there were friends out there, and that someone was asking me to be receptive to something new. I slowly told Grandma what took place, and she blessed the man from afar. A neighbor's servant came to greet us; we were surprised that there was a soul left in Baliwag. There were probably just the three of us in the whole town. He greeted us warmly and said he would get snails (Philippine escargot) and rice for us, and help cook the dinner. He went out to the outer kitchen and started pulling out baskets for his harvest. Grandma and I began to straighten up the house. I set the antique dining table with the beautiful China kept in the house as relics. As I opened up the front *capiz* shell windows, I could see the trail of soldiers still walking by.

In the evening, the officer came with another officer. They were not very talkative, but neither were we. The man servant served the food at the table, and I tried to talk. They wondered what I was doing there. I told them what I could, but felt I was not offering much—the cat had got my tongue. They were polite, enjoyed the ham, the Philippine escargot, garden vegetables, and rice. After dinner, I asked them to make themselves comfortable on the antique wicker divans in the living room. In no time, one was falling asleep. I knew they were quite pleased to have had a homemade meal and a little rest. They thanked us and went back to their troops.

We were equally exhausted, went to bed, and readied ourselves for our walk to Manila the next day. I felt new energy from these men, as though it were coming from Heaven. I wrote a farewell letter to the owners of the house, the Magno family, who offered us the use of their antique ancestral house. I loved this old house, with all the prize furniture in it. The Magno's were still hiding in their place, so no one was around.

At 4:00 am, Grandma and I woke up, and after having a little rice and tea, began our walk to Manila. We would go as fast as we could so that we would get there by nighttime. We were not going to sleep until we got there. Walking beside the soldiers seemed the right thing to do. We had not gone far when a weapons carrier with officers stopped by our side. A Major ordered a soldier to ask us to join them in the carrier. I accepted. The Major said to me that they were going to Manila and asked me where we were going. I said we were going to a house we were occupying behind Santo Tomas Concentration Camp. They said they would have to let us off at Calumpit. I said I truly appreciated what they were doing for us. Then we were all silent. The camaraderie was so brief, I was reminded again that we were still at war! In Calumpit, the Major gave me his name and he took our names. He said General MacArthur was back. I got the impression they were going to meet him. There was some excitement on the road with some kind of road block. It looked as if they were waiting for someone. We were told to get off the road, to watch out for snipers, bombs, artillery shells, and good luck! I felt so thankful. We were back. I felt like God was with us. I looked back one time, and something indeed was happening. But we had our life ahead, and though it was dangerous, we walked on.

By evening we reached our "home," the dormitory on Asturias Street, at the back gate of the 15th century Santo Tomas University, now the concentration camp. The back gate was open. A jeep went in, and it was closed again. We were wondering how we were going to find my grandfather, who was in the camp. We went into our house, realized we had not eaten since that morning, and there was no food in the house at all. We drank lots of water. I wanted Grandma to let me go out and scavenge for food—whatever I might be able to buy. But there was constant shelling from artillery guns a few blocks from us and explosions followed by fire. I thought it would be foolish to go out and decided to go hungry instead. Shortly after, Albert burst into the house. Our reunion was full of joy and fun; we were laughing for no reason. He asked us to sit down and said he had a surprise for us. In a formal quiet ceremony, he took out a package from his pocket and put it in front of us. It was a piece of white bread! It was so precious, we just stared at it, smelling its sacred scent. Then Grandma cut it in four. She and I had one piece each and gave Albert two. I nibbled on mine, trying to reacquaint myself with the taste of wheat. It was more than wheat—it was mana. Our hunger had been so deep. This bread was simply a sign there would be more in the future. All of a sudden, our temporary house felt temporary, and we were headed back to Sta. Ana, where our real home was. The war was over, and a renewal was beginning. I tried to let go of tension but could not yet.

After we parted in Pampanga, Albert had gone with the soldiers to Manila and proceeded to the concentration camp looking for Grandpa. The university gym, where Grandpa was staying with elderly men, had been shelled from Japanese Navy ships in Manila Bay, and he apparently got hit and was taken to an emergency field station. Albert was trying to find out where the emergency station was. He left immediately after our bread ceremony. The following morning I went with Grandma into Santo Tomas and inquired of the army people manning tables where he was. They gave us the location; it was somewhere in Sta. Mesa, pretty far from where we were. Albert saw us and said he had been given a meal and was trying to straighten out Grandpa's papers so he could be legally released from Santo Tomas Concentration Camp.

Grandma and I went back to Asturias. Albert gave us a couple of boiled potatoes from the canteen. Having eaten, we took off for our long walk to the emergency field station in Sta. Mesa. This walk, we knew, could be a very dangerous one. There was no one else around. We were about to cross the Pasig River but saw the south-side of Manila burning. American soldiers were building a pontoon bridge and told us they were not ready, and that we should stay where we are. All the other bridges were bombed. So we took a different route, a longer one, going across abandoned roads, fields where the grass was very high, and a couple of small canals. We did not meet another soul. Occasionally there would be sniper fire and we would take cover behind trees or get down flat on the ground. When we felt safe again, we would continue our walk. Once the smell of gunfire was close and we were afraid there might be Japanese soldiers ready to ambush us, but such was not the case. At a distance I saw a Red Cross sign. We arrived at an old mansion where the emergency station was set up. There were a number of weapons carriers, ambulances, and jeeps outside. Inside it was very orderly and clean. We were given juice right away and taken to Grandpa who was in a room recovering from a heart attack and wounds from shrapnel.

We had not seen him in three and a half years, other than seeing him from outside the Santo Tomas chapel. After much hugging and kissing, all we could do was cry. Then he said that his old partner, Courtney Whitney, who was now a general and an aide to General MacArthur, had just been there to see him. Did we see him? I felt the spirit of the "old boys" come back. My pride swelled. Most of the Filipino hospital staff knew who we were. The Americans were new and did not. It felt as though our old identity was being recovered from the dark. Upon seeing my swollen ankle, the staff washed my wound and gave me sulfas to take. We stayed until after dinner and were transported back to Asturias Street in a jeep. Grandpa was to stay at the emergency station, and we were to go back to our home in Sta. Ana to receive him and the family, who were, by now, probably back in Manila from Barrio Labak and ready to go back home to Sta. Ana.

The walk to Sta. Ana was to be accomplished the following day. Grandma and I woke up again at 4:00 am. This time, we stopped by the Santo Tomas Chapel to give offerings of thanks for all the time we were able to use the chapel, not only for mass but to see Grandpa at a distance while he was interned at the gymnasium. Then we walked down to the Pasig River, past the Malacañan Palace, and onto the pontoon bridge, which was now finished.

At the pontoon bridge, many people were coming north, towards us, escaping the bombings and street killings in the south. We were going south and, again, alone. A couple of soldiers on the pontoon bridge asked why we were so crazy as to do that. I answered that we were going to Sta. Ana and that there seemed to be no fires in that direction. So with good wishes thrown at us, we were allowed to cross. We headed for the Paco Cemetery, avoiding the big fires that engulfed blocks and blocks of the city. There were army vehicles, water trucks, and fire trucks. A little further were soldiers with guns—fighting was still going on. We were stopped by soldiers and brought to an officer, who took down our names and where we were going. We were given water from their canteens. One gave me an American dollar out of his pocket, and another gave us chicklets and a candy bar. Then they directed us where to go to avoid snipers. We were to cross the Paco Canal in an area that was not bombed. The stench of burning flesh and death was around—there were some bodies lying around. All of Paco west of the Canal was gone. From General Luna Street to St. Theresa's College, San Marcelino Church, the Madrigal's house, and the whole of Paco Market—everything was flattened. I could not see beyond that; it was a wall of fire. Everything near the cemetery was leveled, and what was not was still burning. At the Canal, a man had a raft made of bamboo which he used to take people across at a very hefty price. On the other side, Paco was not completely burned yet. We sighed with relief getting to the other side. We did not pass by the ESCO factory. It was a little bit out of the way, and there seemed to be fire there. We found out later that it was burning while we were walking near it on another street. A few people were beginning to do a little commerce—setting up little stands, selling food and firewood. There was no running water. The Army set up emergency water stations for drinking water. We passed by a first aid station and queues for food, which was being given freely by the US Red Cross. There were also trucks passing by with dead people being taken to cemeteries.

We queued at a food line. We were given bread, macadamia nuts, butter and a can of sardines. I was so grateful, and about to cry. I thought of my father, wondering where he was. Was he coming home to surprise us? It was nearly dusk. We were wondering if our house was still there. Seeing the Sta. Ana Church was incredible, but as we went along the bend on Old Panaderos Road, we saw our house at a distance. A man who recognized us came and told us that the Japanese had burned the house just a week before. As we got closer, we could see the blackened carcass of the mansion we once lived in. Steeling ourselves for any surprises, we entered one of the rental houses across the street. It was open; no one was there. My aunt's house was intact, and so was the other rental house. The whole area was completely deserted. We opened windows, and touched the woodwork. The tile floor was wonderfully cool. I took off my blouse and put it on the floor for Grandma to lie down on. A feeling of peace washed through me. We were home.

Figure 1: Picture of Ruth's mother Engracia Hale Cobb with her seven children Frank, Ruth, Grace, Jenny, Willie, Rosemarie, Elmer. Taken in 1940.

Figure 2: Ruth riding a pony beside her dad in the Sta. Ana property, 1937.

Figure 3: Frankie, Ruth, Grace, Jenny and Willie in the Sta. Ana gardens in front of the rattan factories

Figure 4: Engracia Cobb and her children in their country house at Baguio, 1939.

Figure 5: Engracia Cobb with her children Frankie, Ruth, Grace, Jenny, Willie, Rosemarie and Elmer. This was the last picture taken in San Juan at the home of Father-in-law Ira Cobb, 1941.

Figure 6: Teodora Hale and her grandchildren in Baguio, 1941. Last photo taken before WWII.

Figure 7: Ira Dee Cobb with all his children in San Juan, Philippines after the funeral of his wife, 1932.

Figure 8: First grade class photo Central School Elementary section of H.A. Bordner, Taft Ave Manila. Teacher is Mrs. Miller. Ruth is seated second from the left, 1940.

Figure 9: Third Grade class photo Central School, Elementary section of H.A. Bordner, Taft Ave., Manila. Ruth is first row standing seventh from the left. Teacher is Mrs. Sylvester, 1938.

...ie Wheeler celebrates birthday last Sunday afternoon. His guest includes: Erlinda
...n and Peter Quijano, Vivian Ellis, James Murphy, Leopold and Marvin Hess, Ruth
...rank Hale Cobb, Helen Anderson, Bobbie Murphy, Henry Elzingre, Carmencita Fa-
...Jackson, James and Roderick Hall, Tommy and Patrick Spiers, Esperancita and Juan
...astro, Carol May and Eugene Lee Dyson, and Pinky Wheeler.

Figure 10: Birthday party that included Ruth and Frank Hale Cobb. Ruth is second row, second from the right, circa 1938.

Figure 11: Rosemarie, Jenny, their cousin Marlene, Frank, kneeling in front, Willie and Elmer Cobb. House in the background was the Hale house and it was used by the Japanese Army as an Officers' Club and was burned a week before liberation. Photo taken by Louis Cobb, U.S. Merchant Marine 1945.

Figure 12: Frank Hale with Philippine Senators at the Malacanan Palace, January 15, 1940.

Figure 13: Frank H. Hale with Manuel Luis Quezón, a Filipino statesman, soldier, and politician who served as president of the Commonwealth of the Philippines from 1935 to 1944.

Ruth Hale Cobb Hill

provincial board of Tayabas, has been twice elected representative from the second district of that province and in 1931, appointed provincial governor of Tayabas in 1928 until he has been elected as Provincial Governor. Six months after his election as governor he was appointed Under-Secretary of the Department of the Interior and Labor.

Secretary Guinto, while he was governor of Tayabas, organized the powerful League of Provincial Governors and became its first president.

FRANK H. HALE

To be a Filipino we do not merely mean that one must be brown in color, born here, and has sympathy for his fellow countrymen. For adopted sons can be dubbed Filipinos too, if they have stayed here in the Islands long enough and shown tendencies to become one among Filipinos, working with them for the common good of all.

Such is the case with Frank H. Hale, president of the Hale Shoe Company, manufacturers of the famous Esco Shoes. He has been in the Islands more than thirty-six years, has worked with the Filipinos, and gained their confidence by acting and being one of them, helping them and doing perhaps what few other Filipinos would ever do: trust his million-peso concern to a group of Filipinos, his able and trusted employees.

Frank H. Hale was born in Powell County, Kansas, on August 30, 1880, the son of George Washington Hale and Mary Jane Stradley Hale. He was educated in the grammar school of his own country, after which he entered the "university of hard knocks" in place of college education. During the Spanish-American War, he joined the American forces which were sent to the Islands in 1900, and he has remained here ever since.

Soon after the expiration of his term of service, he started making shoes in a shack in McKinley, which he later on organized into what is now commonly known as the Hale Shoe Co., manufacturers of the famous Esco shoes. From the very beginning Mr. Hale has been guiding the destiny of this company until it has reached its present position of being the largest leather shoe factory in the Orient and which has a capacity of turning out 1,500 pairs of shoes every day.

Mr. Hale has great confidence in the ability of the Filipinos. In proof of this he has placed the management of the firm into the hands of his employees who are all Filipinos. Due to his varied business enterprises, naturally he could not devote all of his time to one particular business, and so he lets his Filipino employees take care of the shoe factory.

Aside from being the head of the Hale Shoe Company, he is also the president of the Lyric Music House, of the Rattan Products Mfg., Co., Philippine Fiber Products Inc. and the Gold River Mining Co.

Member: American Chamber of Commerce, Wack Wack Golf Club, Fraternity of Masons, 32nd degree Shriner, Knights of Phytias.

He is married to Teodora Elasigue with whom he has two children: Christina, 33, and Engracia, 32.

WILLIAM W. HARRIS

William W. Harris, mining magnate and former manager of the Negros-Philippine Lumber Corporation, was born in Indianapolis, Indiana, on September 28, 1872, son of George S. and Elizabeth S. (Noble) Harris. He is essentially a product of the public schools of his native state.

Shortly after the completion of his studies, he went to Hawaii, where he became associated with Lewers & Cooke. Ltd., of Honolulu, the largest hardware and lumber firm in the Hawaiian Islands. In this company he remained for more than seventeen years, after which he came to the Philippines, arriving at Manila on January 20, 1913. From the year of his arrival up to 1918, he served as assistant manager of the Insular Lumber Company. Then in 1919 he became general manager of the Negros-Philippine Lumber Company, which post he held until very recently.

Eighty-nine

Figure 14a: Frank H. Hale's entry in the social register 1936.

The Walk: My Journey of Survival of the Japanese Military Occupation of Manila

(SOCIAL REGISTER)

ADRIAN GOT

GUILLERMO B. GUEVARA

LEON G. GUINTO

FRANK H. HALE

Eighty-three

Figure 14b: Frank H. Hale's entry in the social register 1936.

46

Press. By the late Twenties, however, Hale was the biggest of the shoe manufacturers. In 1928, he made a trip to the United States to purchase new machinery, and his reactions not only shed light on the Protestant work-and-save ethic which had been transplanted to the Philippines, but anticipated depression adjustments. According to Robb, who did an excellent article[11] on him in 1933, Hale was appalled by the extravagant living that he saw at home:

> In New York he could find no businessman at his office before 10 o'clock, and 11 o'clock might be too late to see him; business was running at such a volume that men seemed to believe it would come to them without attention. You had to cool your heels in an outer office to wait to give a man an order and write him out your check.

> Girls in Akron were getting $35 and $40 a week at the tire plants, men's wages were on an unheard-of scale. At one factory a pair of girls stood beside a conveyor and brushed colors, red and blue, into the trademark stamped into the edge of the tires; these girls got $72 a week; they were style artists.... Women's fine apparel shops and jewelry stores were the principal emporia along main thoroughfares. On a Saturday afternoon Hale saw a mob fighting to get into a jewelry store, the police on the job....these people, mostly girls, were only trying to get into the store to pay the weekly installments on their jewels....that store...was stocked, to his astonished enlightenment, with rare diamonds costing as high as $7000 apiece.

To a hard-working Yankee reared in the austere tenets of the Christian Church, his home country was obviously headed for trouble. Hale therefore returned to the Philippines without placing his orders, determined to prepare for the economic storm which his visit had convinced him lay ahead. When the depression struck the Philippines, he was ready for it. In May 1933, his factory was running at full capacity, his accounts receivable were no problem (he gave little credit; most of his Chinese distributors preferred cash discounts), and he was poised to expand as soon as the depression lifted. In the meantime, he continued to work the same long hours as he always had, spending most of his time in his shop, dressed like any of his workingmen:

> It is notorious in Manila that Hale is a glutton for work; he himself says that holidays are his longest

Figure 15a: Write up of the Hale Shoe company.

days; even on an Easter trip to Baguio he is like a ship in the doldrums: he likes work days, full sail ahead, now at the factory, now at his retail stores, now at the bank. In personal habits he makes an ideal success-story subject: no drinking, no tobacco, no whiling away time at clubs; but strict domesticity, rising at dawn, at the factory at 7 o'clock, and at 6:30 in the afternoon, far after the cocktail hour, closing his Escolta store and giving the clerks a lift home.

I have to give my business close attention [Hale says].... It would go to pieces if I didn't. Now mind you, I think I have a good organization,.... but it always pays for the "old man" himself to be on the job and see what's doing. Besides I like it. I've worked all my life, and I always will.

In 1933, Hale, who had lived behind his factory for twenty years, had begun to build a fine, modern home for his wife and two daughters on 14 acres overlooking the Pasig River at Santa Ana, and Robb, without making the specific point, noted how this typical American Old Timer, though guided by traditional, unrelenting ideas of hard and conscientious work, had nonetheless adapted to the prevailing paternalistic atmosphere which characterized the Philippine industrial scene until the last years of the Commonwealth:

The nostalgic influence of a rural boyhood drives Hale on, making the most of the spacious grounds. One building will be a recreational hall for his employees. At present a floor in the factory office building is used for this purpose. There are occasional social gatherings and evening dances and one grand annual ball. The detail of a flattering espirit de corps among the company's personnel is by no means neglected; thus organized athletics, the Esco baseball team and Esco basketball team, and the next venture in footwear will be sports shoes.

Hale's philosophy was the key to his victory over the depression, but it would betray him when labor troubles came in 1939. Encouraged by President Quezon's inflammatory public statements (which led to strikes at three American oil companies), extreme demands put forth by their workers led both Hale and McGrath to shut down their factories, — in the case of McGrath, permanently.

Figure 15b: Write up of the Hale Shoe company.

Figure 16a: Advertising for the Hale Shoe Company pre WWII.

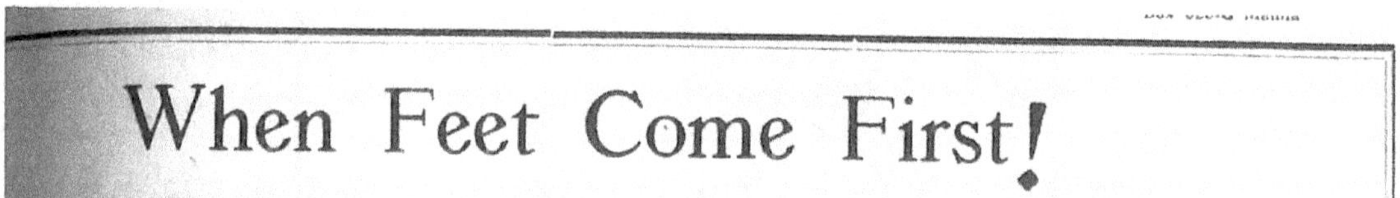

If you want
to look good—

wear

ESCO

SHOES!

City chaps look smart 'cause they know how to dress the part. But you don't need to be a city guy to wear snappy footwear 'cause in any town all thruout the Philippine Islands, there is always an ESCO dealer 'round the corner.

ESCO SHOE STORES
615 Escolta and 333 Legarda

When Feet Come First!

Ravishing beauties with the famous "school-girl complexion" and flawless attire — *still look upon their feet to carry them over.*

However, it's not fancy alone that carries weight in the selection of their footwear—what with upset fortunes in this topsy-turvy world, most anybody has to consider too the exacting demands of the purse strings.

All things being equal—*smartness, quality, style*—who wouldn't prefer an ESCO when anybody can easily afford three or four pairs at a time.

ESCO SHOE STORES
615 Escolta and 333 Legarda

Figure 16b: Advertising for the Hale Shoe Company pre WWII.

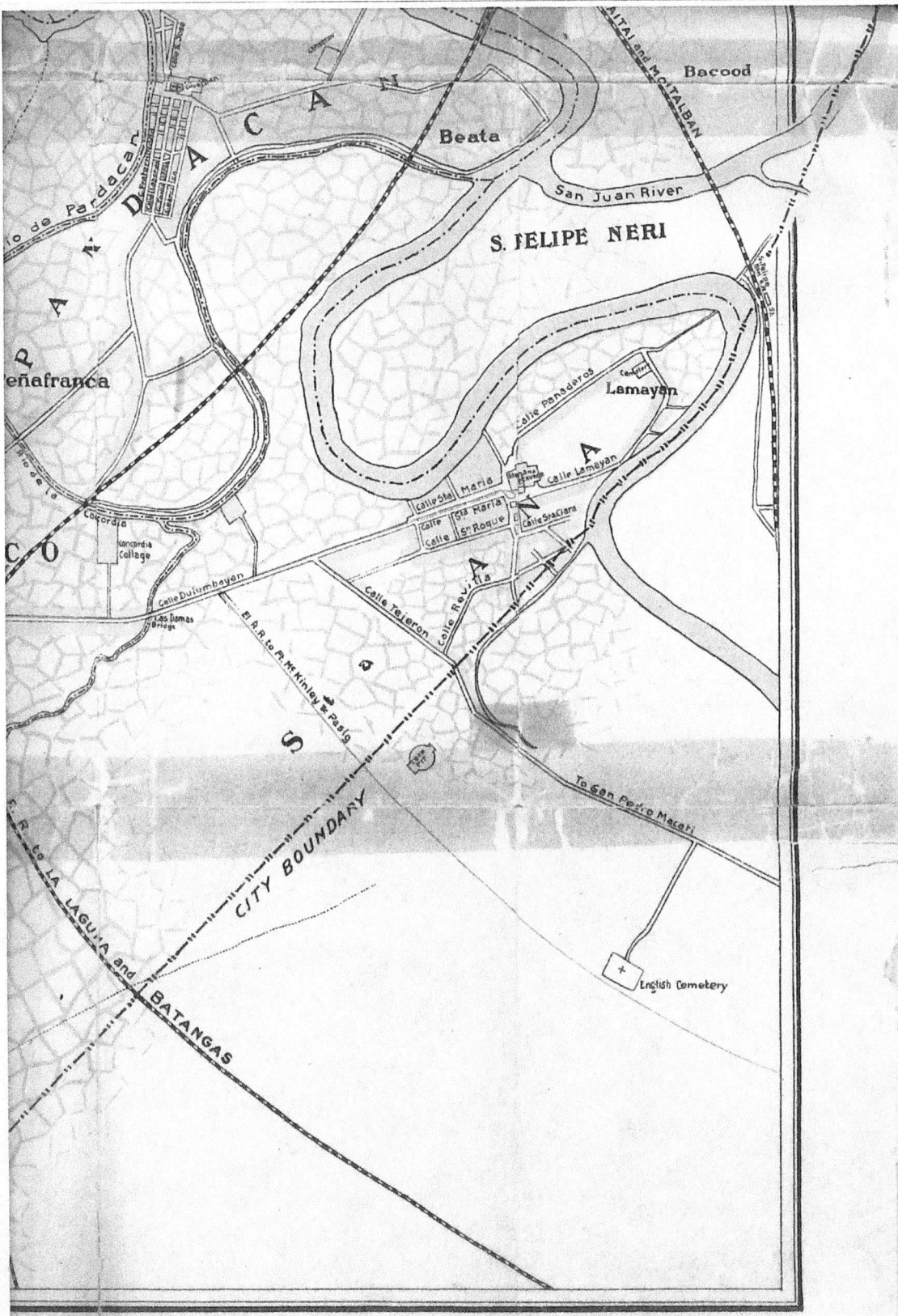

Figure 17: Map of Old Manila showing location of the home of Frank Hale and the rattan factories on Old Panaderos Road.

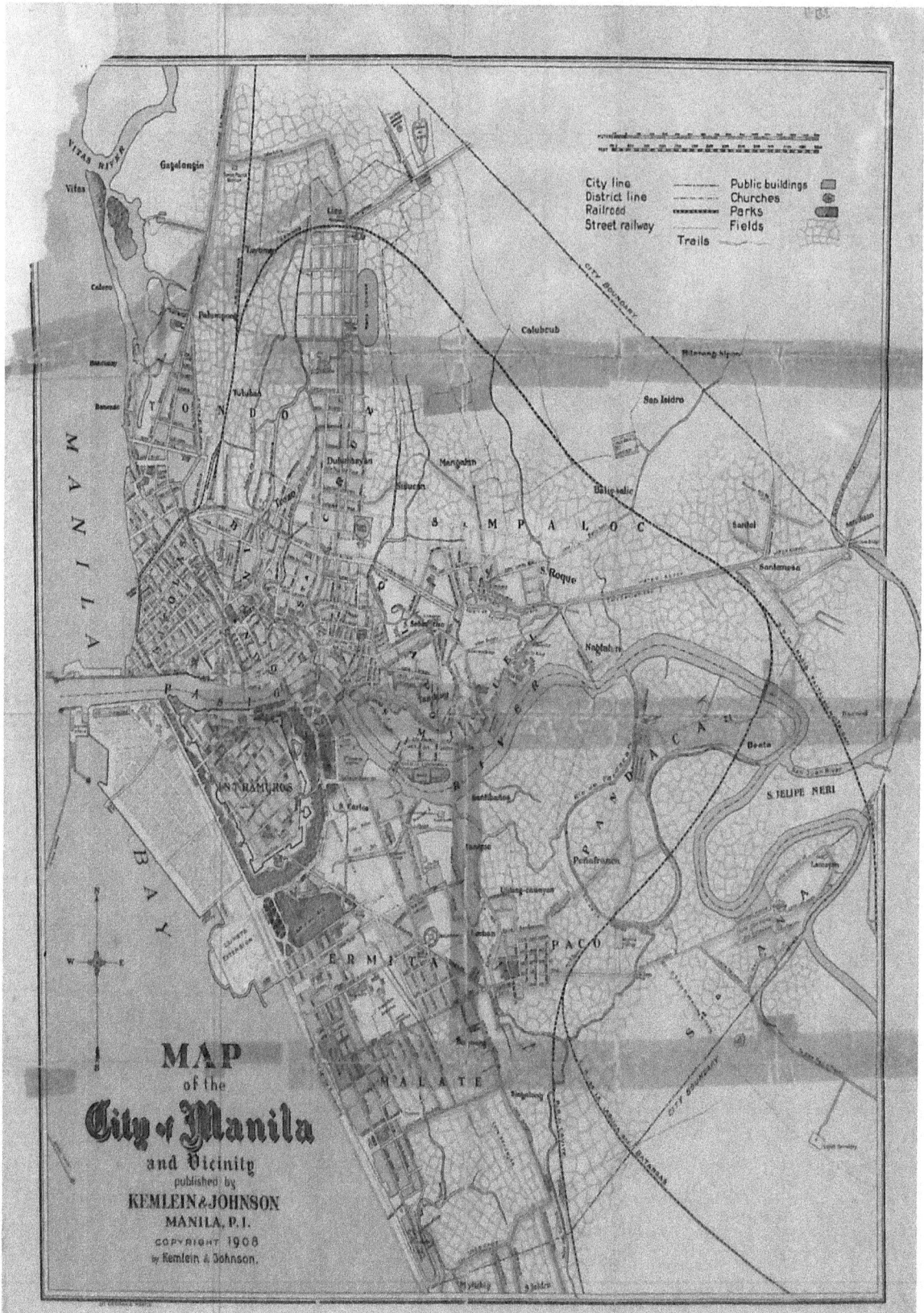

Figure 18: Map of City of Manila 1908, Published by Kemlein and Johnson.

XIV ANNIVERSARY

The Tribune

Hale Shoe COMPANY

THEN and NOW

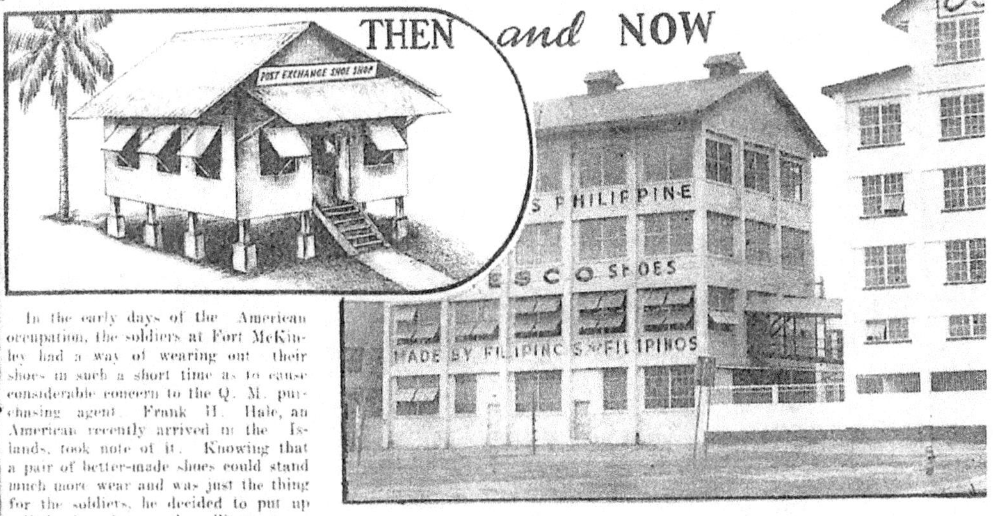

POST EXCHANGE SHOE SHOP

PHILIPPINE

ESCO SHOES

MADE BY FILIPINOS FILIPINOS

In the early days of the American occupation, the soldiers at Fort McKinley had a way of wearing out their shoes in such a short time as to cause considerable concern to the Q. M. purchasing agent. Frank H. Hale, an American recently arrived in the Islands, took note of it. Knowing that a pair of better-made shoes could stand much more wear and was just the thing for the soldiers, he decided to put up a little shoe shop on the military reservation. This was in 1906. The little shop was an immediate success.

By 1912 Mr. Hale decided to expand and asked a few friends in with him to form a corporation. Under the name of Exchange Shoe Company they produced the first machine-made Esco shoes. The factory was a modest frame plant in Paco, Manila, and at the time, Mr. Hale had only eight men working for him.

Today the factory employs some 400 men in a group of concrete buildings, where 1,500 pairs of Esco shoes are manufactured each day. Even in the early days when Mr. Hale was cutting and sewing leather by hand, he had visions of a great industry and stores, and part of every peso he made was invested in the development of his factory. By 1920 he had acquired the controlling stock in the corporation, and though he kept the Esco trade name, the firm became known as the **Hale Shoe Company.**

When Mr. Frank H. Hale saw how the American soldiers at Fort McKinley easily wore out their shoes, he decided to do something about it. So in 1916 he erected a little shoe shop, above left, on the military reservation.

time to attend club meetings. Though a member of the Wack Wack Country Club he still has to play his first round of golf. He only has time for work. But he sees to it that his employees get the benefit of relaxation that he

The entire factory is operated by Filipinos. Each department is under the supervision of a Filipino foreman; and indicative of the advancement of some of the employees is the case of its superintendent, Agripino Ramos, who started as a tack boy in the early Esco days. The Company is very proud of its slogan, "Esco shoes are made by Filipinos for everybody."

Beside the million-peso plant at 479 Canonigo, Paco, the **Hale Shoe Company** has a store on the Escolta and another at Calle Legarda. Dealers represent it throughout the Philippines.

Its half-a-million-peso machinery outfit is of the latest "Lightning Line" type. The ₱300,000 materials stored in the ₱250,000 buildings make the Hale Shoe Company not only the pioneer but also the biggest factory in the

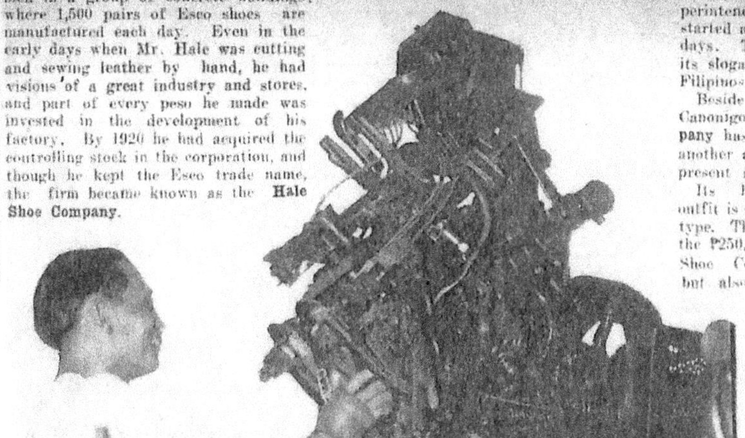

Left: Factory hand of the Hale Shoe Company operating a modern machine which, because of its special design, is used only for first class leather shoes. This is one only of the 220 devices used in the factory for turning out quality shoes.

8/9/2010

Figure 19: Fourteenth anniversary of The Tribune (Manila) with an article of the Hale Shoe Company describing history then and now.

The American Historical Collection (AHC), established in 1950, consists of 13,518 books, 18,674 photographs, and other materials related to the American experience in the Philippines and the relationship of the two countries. With the possible exception of the holdings of the U.S. Library of Congress, the AHC is the largest, most diverse, and most complete collection of materials of this kind in the world.

In 1950, U.S. Ambassador Myron Cowen, who saw the devastation wrought by the Second World War on many things including the memory of the times preceding it, encouraged the American community to donate books and other materials pertaining to the first half of the 20th century. His initiative was responsible for the early phase of the collection.

Acquisitions, donations, and funds were administered by the American Historical Committee.

The American Historical Collection Foundation, Inc. aids and supports the AHC.

Ownership of the AHC is in trust with the American Association of the Philippines.

Filipinos and Americans are encouraged to donate appropriate books toward the development of this great collection.

3L Rizal Library Special Collections Building
Ateneo de Manila University
Loyola Heights, Quezon City
1108 Philippines

Telefax :(632) 426-6001 ext. 5567
E-mail: ahc@admu.edu.ph

Website: http://rizal.lib.admu.edu.ph/ahc

Library Hours:

Monday-Friday 8:00 a.m.- 5:00 p.m.
Saturday   8:00 a.m. - 12:00 nn.

American Historical Collection

Presents

Notable Americans in the Philippines and Donors to the AHC

On exhibit
June – December 2012

W. Cameron Forbes — Eugene A. Perkins — Leonard G. Dawson

David T. Sternberg — Frank F. Hale

These donors individually made their mark in Phil-Am history. They contributed to shaping the nation as Governor-General (Forbes); as a Manila lawyer, a mason, and a bibliophile (Perkins); as government treasurer (Dawson); as a guru in Manila (Sternberg); and as a pioneer shoe manufacturer (Hale).

William Cameron Forbes
Governor-general, 1909-1913

The W. Cameron Forbes Collection is the single most valuable donation to the Collection. The collection consists of document serial pieces and non-official books about the Philippine Islands. The government publications include annual reports of officials and departments, U.S.-Philippine Commission Reports and Journals, the Official Gazette, the Executive Orders, and a set of Public Laws.

Eugene A. Perkins
Manila's lawyer, a mason, and a bibliophile

Comparable in importance to that of the Forbes Collection is the Eugene A. Perkins Collection. The Perkins collection is rich in ephemera, embracing early and late Spanish-Philippines items.

It is also rich in government publications and official documents of the American period (1898-1935), particularly in periodicals and pamphlets and other publications of the United States Congress, especially hearings on political and economic affairs between the two countries. The Commonwealth period (1935-1946, except 1942-1945) is also well-represented.

Leonard G. Dawson
Provincial treasurer

Mr. Leonard G. Dawson, served as provincial treasurer of several provinces — Ilocos, Tayabas, Pangasinan, Leyte, Albay, and Iloilo — in the early 1900's.

A valuable addition to the holdings to the AHC is the Leonard Geeding Dawson Collection. The donation was made by his widow, Helen Dwyer Dawson. Mrs. Dawson came to the Philippines as a public school teacher assigned in Ilocos province. The Dawson Collection is particularly strong in the middle and late Spanish period, but it also includes a wide selection from the early American era in the Philippines.

Collection of
LEONARD G. DAWSON
Donated by
HELEN D. DAWSON

David T. Sternberg
Guru in Manila

According to Father Miguel Bernad, SJ, Sternberg was a great American and a true friend of the Philippines. Most of the books from the Sternberg collection deal with Philippine-American relations. The collection is also rich in Southeast Asian books.

A frequently borrowed book from the donation is the "Philippine Pseudonyms, Aliases, Pen Names, Screen Names, and Names Aberrations (1967)."

Frank F. Hale
Pioneer shoe manufacturer

Hale came to the Philippines with the U. S. Army as a civilian employee in 1898 and rose to become one of the pioneering industrialists in the country. He was the proprietor of the Hale Shoe Company.

Ruth Hale Cobb Hill donated to the AHC her grandfather's memorabilia items – a leather suitcase, a pair of shoes, a brass instrument, a tin suitcase (used by the US Army, ca. 1898), a leather briefcase with inscription "F.H. Hale," and other mementos.

Figure 20a, 20b: Write up of Frank H. Hale for the American Historical Collection Exhibition of notable Americans in the Philippines June-Dec 2012.

FRANK H. HALE

Old timer, industrialist, and friend of the Filipino people

At the time of his death in Manila in 1952, pioneer shoe manufacturer of the Philippines, Frank H. Hale [b. Aug. 30, 1872] was called "Friend of the Filipino People." He was also known as "Mang Isko" by millions of Filipinos, who gave him this nickname in appreciation of his contribution to Filipino life. His vision was that every Filipino replaced his or her *chinelas* with a pair of sturdy, stylish, and affordable shoes. The brand *Esco* became a household word, and its shoes were soon being worn even in remote areas of the Philippines. Mr. Hale became the largest exporter of shoes to the U. S. and Europe. At the outbreak of WWII, *Esco* was the largest manufacturer of shoes in the Philippines and, according to some economists, possibly in the whole of Asia.

From humble beginnings as a volunteer cobbler with the U. S. Army aboard one of the American ships sailing to the Philippines in 1898, followed by his setting up shop in Fort McKinley under the auspices of General Pershing, Hale built what became *Esco*. Having grown up on a wheat farm in California that suffered from a wheat market disaster in the U. S., he was determined to create something needed in the Philippines to last for generations to come and to be a stable organization staffed by Filipinos for Filipinos. Reinvesting all profits made, he turned the cobbler shop into a modern industry. He arranged for machinery, backed by royalties, to be brought from United Shoe Manufacturing in Boston, Massachusetts, and imported the finest leathers from the U. S., Italy,

Hale's shop in Fort McKinnley

Figure 20c: Write up of Frank H. Hale for the American Historical Collection Exhibition of notable Americans in the Philippines, June-Dec 2012.

Argentina and Australia, to manufacture fine shoes capable of competing worldwide in terms of style and strength. *Esco* became the manufacturer for leading brands in the U. S. and Europe, as well as the contractor for military and industrial shoes in the Philippines.

Manpowered by 100% Filipino skilled workers, *Esco* became a model corporation where employees were given housing, medical, social and sports facilities. Employees' families thrived, and some opened up their own businesses backed by *Esco* resources.

Hale then experimented with Philippine materials, opening Tropicraft Corporation, which experimented steel and plastics to increase the strength and life rattan furniture. His admiration of the Philippines led him to call it the "Land of Promise, Opportunity." He was included in *Who's Who* with other leaders of agriculture and industry in the Philippines. He also opened Lyric Music House, bringing in the finest musical instruments from abroad for the tastes of talented musicians of the Philippines.

During WWII, the Japanese military government confiscated the factories and turned them to their own uses. Mr. Hale was interned in Santo Thomas where he helped sew up older co-interns' shoes. Reconstruction after the war meant adjusting to new conditions within the new Philippine Republic. He was weak by then but nevertheless returned to success but on a smaller scale.

The exhibit features Mr. Hale's personal belongings, generously donated by his granddaughter Ruth Hale Cobb Hill to the American Historical Collection.

American Historical Collection
3rd Level Rizal Library Special Collections Building
Ateneo de Manila University, Loyola Heights
Quezon City, 1108 Philippines
Telefax: (632) 426-6001 loc. 5567
Email: ahc@admu.edu.ph
Website: http://rizal.lib.admu.edu.ph/ahc

Library Hours: Mon-Fri 8:00 a.m.-5:00 p.m.; Sat 8:00 a.m.-12:00 nn.

Figure 20d: Write up of Frank H. Hale for the American Historical Collection Exhibition of notable Americans in the Philippines, June-Dec 2012.

Figure 21: Hale Family estate in Sta. Ana with Ruth's mother's house (back left), Main House (center) and five rattan factory buildings (right). Photo: Intramuros Administration.

Malate Church and Convent, nineteenth century. Courtesy Malate Church.

PARANAQUE   241

Figure 22: Malate Church and convent, 19th century. Courtesy of Malate Church. Ira D. Cobb was interned at Remedios Hospital on the grounds of the former convent in 1942. Remedios Hospital was an extension of the Santo Tomas concentration camp.

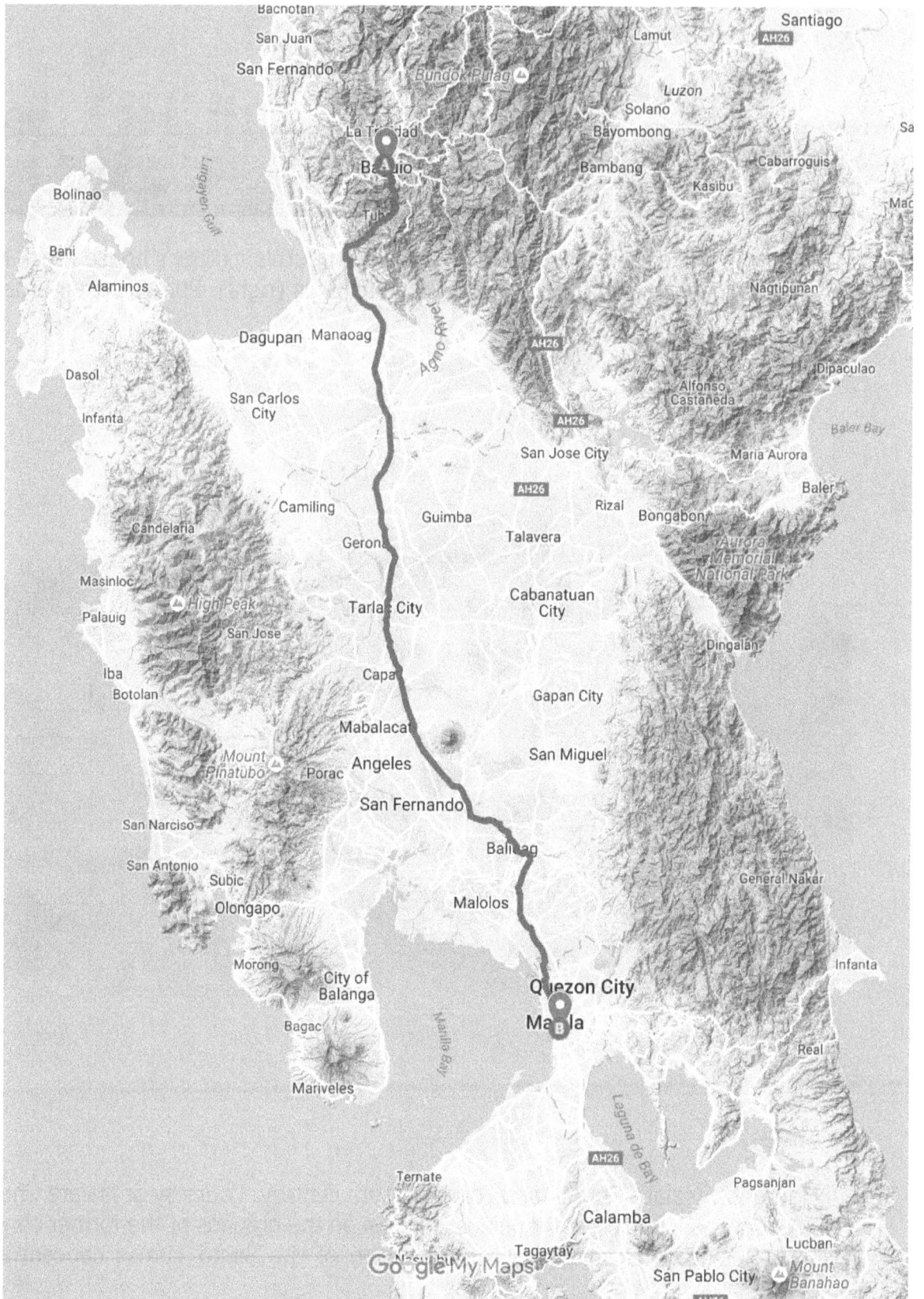

Figure 23a: Google map of Ruth's approximate path from Manila to Baguio with her grandmother going to the Hale Country House. The house was built in 1913. The Hale Family spent every summer in Baguio.

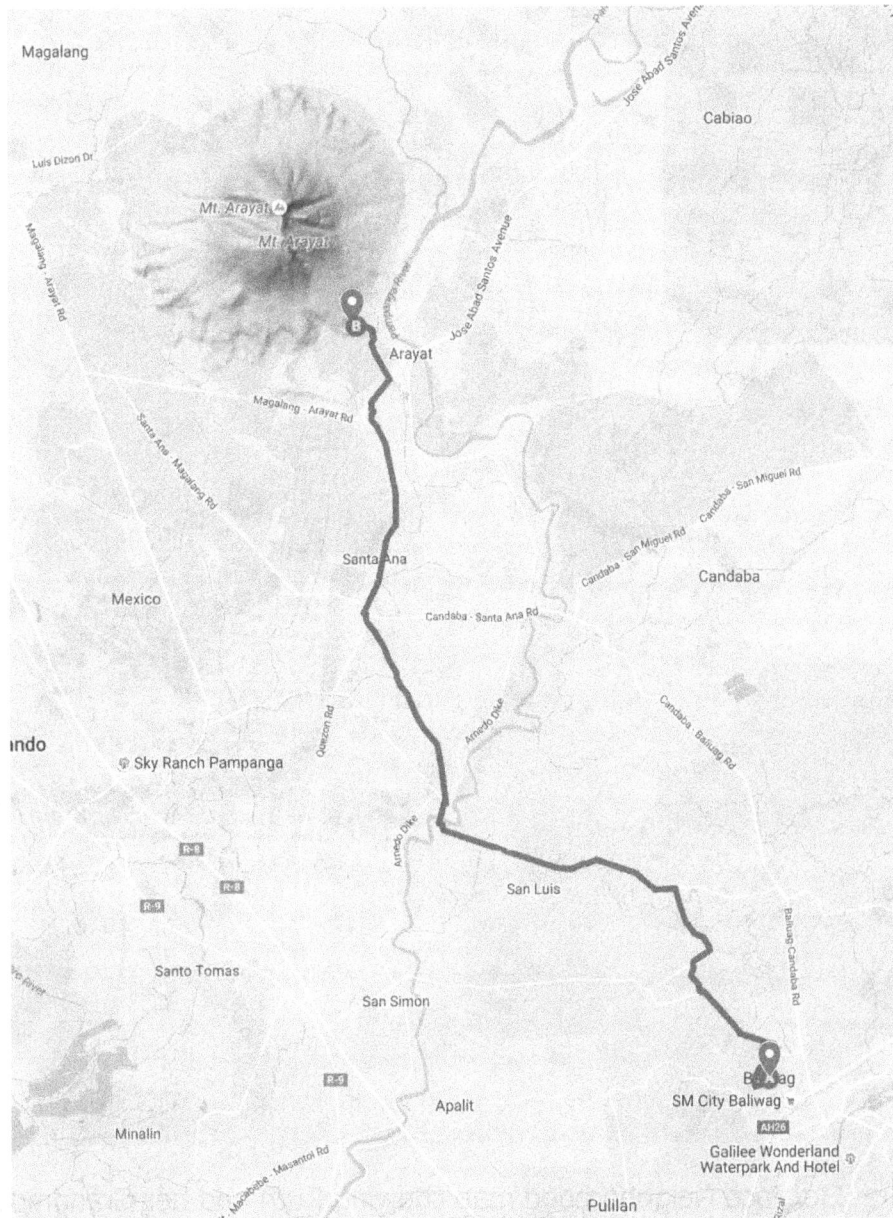

Figure 23b: Google map of Ruth's approximate path walking from Baliuag to Mt. Arayat with her grandmother and the Hukbalahap guerillas. They kept off the roads, walking through rice patties, through San Simon and San Luis, skirting Candaba and continuing through more rice patties to Bario Labak at the foot of Mt. Arayat, near the Pampanga River. Candaba was still considered too dangerous after the massacre.

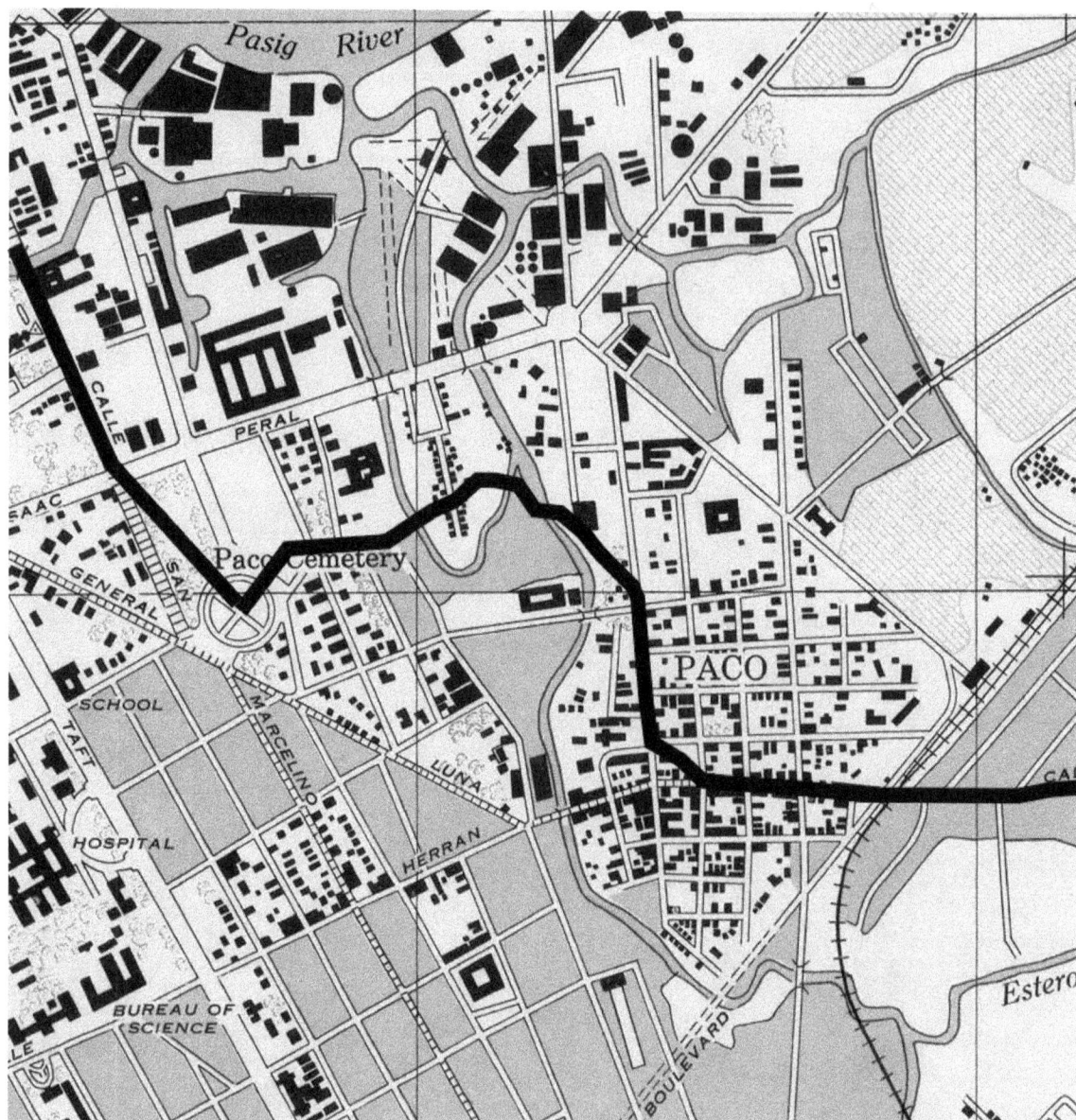

Figure 23c. Paco Neighborhood map showing Ruth and her Grandmother's walking path past the destruction in Intramuros, through the Paco Cemetery, across the canals and streets of Paco and down Calle Herran as they were heading home during the Battle of Manila. US Army map, 1945.

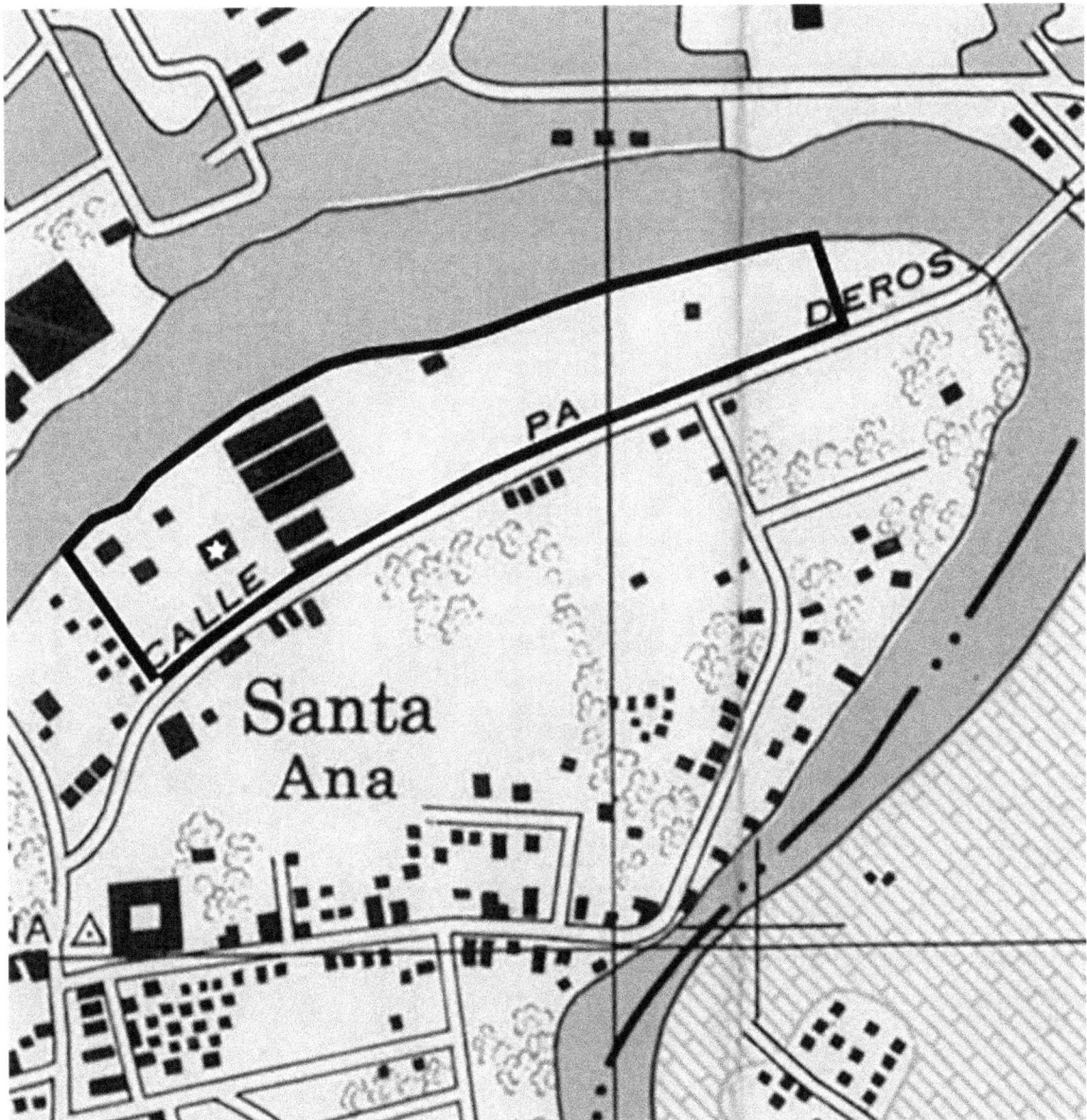

Figure 23d. Sta. Ana Neighborhood map showing the Hale Family property on Calle Old Panaderos, five rattan factories (large buildings in center-left of property), Main House (star), barn (small building directly behind Main House), Play House (left building) and Ruth's Mother's House (upper left corner). The large building next to the survey point symbol triangle is the Church and the group of small buildings across the street is the Sta. Ana Market. U.S. Army map, 1945.

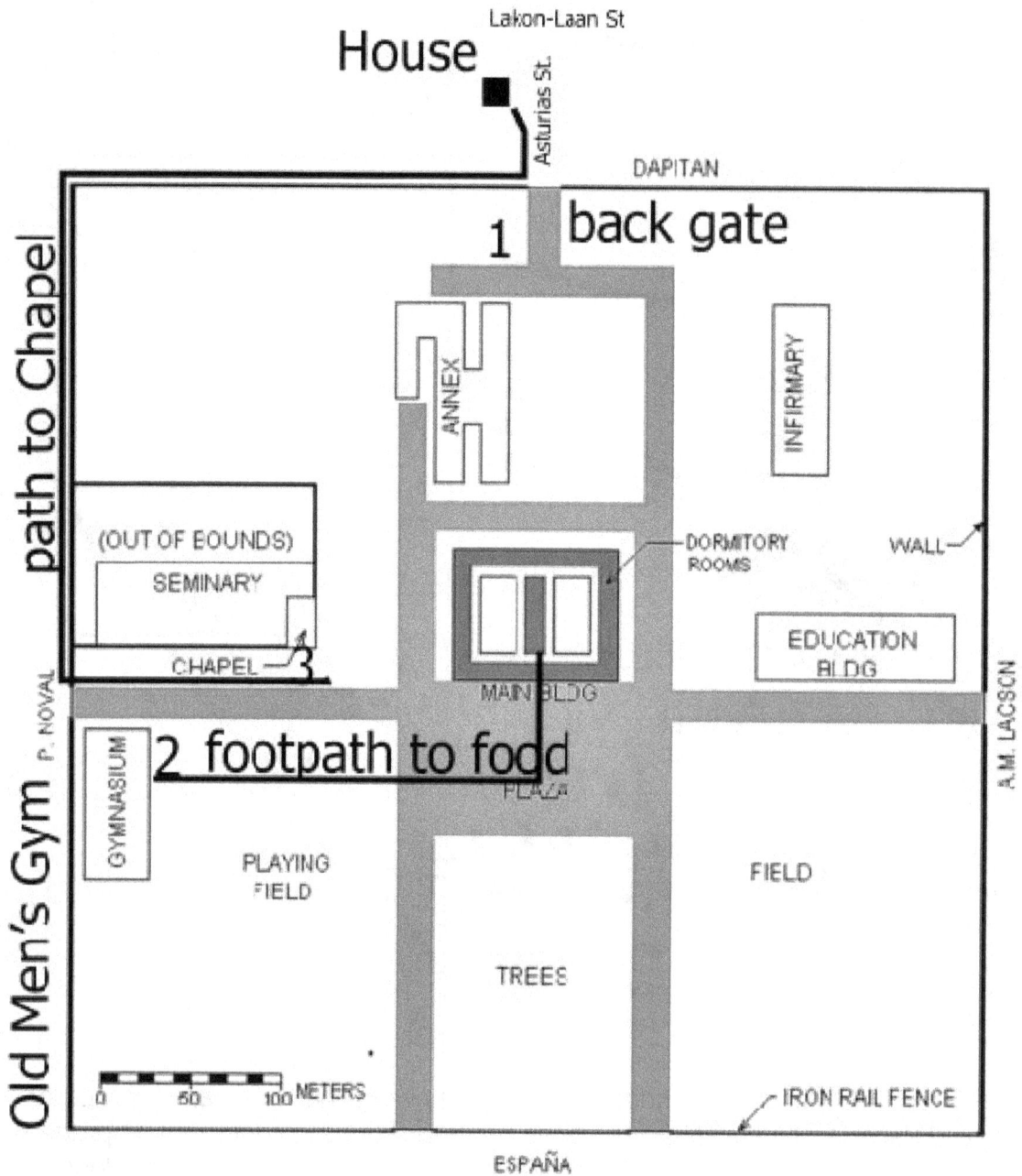

Figure 23e. Santo Tomas Concentration Camp map showing Ruth's path from their house on Asturias Street to the Chapel to see her Grandfather (1, 3) as he would go from the Old Men's Gymnasium to the Main Building for food (2). Base drawing: www.pinterest.com map.

Figure 24: The Hale country house on Legarda Road, Baguio, circa 1915.

Figure 25: Ruth Hale Cobb Hill

Figure 26: The Lyric Music House in Escolta, Manila during a Sunday afternoon accordion demonstration in 1938. Owned by the industrialist Frank H. Hale, with partner General Courtney Whitney, it imported musical instruments from all over the world.

Figure 27: ESCO Hale Shoe Company on Canonigo Street in Paco, Manila, 1941. Frank H. Hale, the company founder, supported the Philippine home industry as advertised on the side of its buildings.

Figure 28: The facade of the ESCO shoe store on Escolta St., Manila, 1940.

Figure 29: Ruins of the Hale Shoe Company, Paco, Manila, 1945. Frank H. Hale donning his apron to start working again as a cobbler after the war. The gentleman next to him is a business associate from the United States.

Figure 30: Ruins of the Hale Shoe Company, Paco, Manila, 1945.

Figure 31: Ruins of the Hale Shoe Company, Paco, Manila, 1945.

Figure 32: Ruins of the Hale Shoe Company, Paco, Manila, 1945.

Back Cover Photograph Historical Notes

Before World War II, the Hale Shoe Company, manufacturer of the famous "Esco" Shoes, situated on the former Canonigo Street in the district of Paco, Manila, was a compound of white concrete and steel buildings. Manufacturing a thousand pairs of shoes daily, it had several warehouses used for the storage of boxed shoes for both inter-island and international export. These warehouses were air-tight, allowing no moisture to come in, for the preservation of their contents. They were also free from natural light in order to preserve lettering and colors on the containers. Electric lights and fans were used.

In 1941, at the beginning of WWII, the company, along with all of its factory buildings, was confiscated by the Japanese Military and converted to the manufacture of shoes for their troops. In their retreat from the advancing American Liberation Forces in February 1945, the factory buildings were included in their burning of the entire south side of Manila. The devastated buildings, pocked by mortar shells and bullets, were now blackened but still standing. There was gnarled metal from destroyed and burned machinery, galvanized roofs, and window frames. Broken glass and ashes covered the grounds.

Following a cleanup in preparation for restoration, some buildings were found to need less structural repair. A few had concrete second and third floors, which, although burned, served as roofs to the floors beneath them. One, the northeast warehouse building, was cleared particularly well. Informants claim that it had been used by American soldiers as quarters during the period of the fighting.

In its interior, a GI had painted portraits of President Franklin D. Roosevelt and President Harry S. Truman on supporting concrete columns of the large space *(back cover photographs)*. On other columns and walls, he had painted pinup girls, in an amateur version of the very popular Varga girls[1] who must have filled their dreams and were emblematic of the women to whom these soldiers hoped to go home.

Our artist represented the women he had come across in daily life: a gal in a uniform, in a cabaret, in an office, or next door. He first sketched the figures with fine brushes against solid white backgrounds, which he then overlaid with thicker paint, most likely bought from the Army PX or sent by family from the U.S. Their simplicity made the figures stand out evocatively, which was intentional. As little light infiltrated the space, except that coming through a mortar hole, the color of the paintings endured. Much can be said for the quality of the paint used.

After WWII, the warehouse was used in relation to various manufacturing needs. No effort was made to restore the paintings, and some damage occurred through water seepage. Damage was further done by an occasional worker imposing his own graffiti on a couple of the paintings. Another source of damage was the crumbling of the concrete. The original building was built in 1912. These paintings were never exhibited publicly. The intent of the artist to entertain his fellow soldiers is preserved in time in the warehouse. In the wake of the building's sale sixty-seven years later, the murals were photographed. With the encouragement of people who were invited to inspect the paintings, Ruth Hale Cobb Hill, the granddaughter of the company's founder and Martoni Ortigas, Director of the Filipinas Heritage Library of the Ayala Museum, engaged in a preservation project. The photographs chosen are by Heritage Library staff photographer Jaime Martinez.

[1] Alberto Vargas was a famous and prolific pin-up artist of the war years. Esquire Magazine dubbed his pin-ups "Varga girls.."

"Lady in Blue" painted in the ESCO Factory by WWII America Army GI

Index

www.ingramcontent.com/pod-product-compliance
Lightning Source LLC
Chambersburg PA
CBHW081156090426
42736CB00017B/3349